A Love of
Nature
in
Paint and Print

Written and Illustrated
by
Bernard Kear

To my wife Pauline with whom I shared many of these experiences and for her patience and practical help and advice and also to my daughters Kathryn and Andrea.

Foreword

I first met Bernard in 1991. I had just been appointed head of Gloucestershire Education Authority's two Environmental Education Centres in the Forest of Dean - the Wilderness Residential Field Study Centre and the Plump Hill Environmental Education Centre. The previous Director of the service, Brian Cave, had appointed Bernard as one of the field studies teachers, on a secondment from the local Drybrook County Primary School. I was new to the Forest of Dean, but it did not take me long to discover that Bernard had been justifiably head hunted for his post, mainly because of his intimate knowledge of the natural history of the Forest and an enviable ability to share his sense of awe and wonder for nature with primary school children. This was happening at a time when children were beginning to exhibit, in ever increasing numbers, an almost phobic fear of nature, due to an upbringing often devoid of close encounters with nature or a reduced exposure to it through outdoor play.

Bernard was born in the Forest of Dean in 1936. He attended the local primary school in Viney Hill and went on to study at Lydney Grammar School. After working in industry, Bernard retrained to become a teacher and went on to spend his entire teaching career as a primary school teacher in the Forest of Dean.

This succinct biography forms a backdrop to the lifelong passion he has for nature - a lifetime of perfecting the inquiring and observational skills of a natural scientist, the eye for descriptive detail of a skilled artist and the communication skills of a professional teacher.

This book is written in Bernard's own words and drawn by his own hand, in such a way as to convey the personal and intimate relationship he has had with the natural world he has spent his lifetime communing with. It's a publication that might have been committed to a dusty shelf if the publisher, David Harris, and Bernard's wife Pauline, his family and friends had not encouraged this self effacing, modest, retired teacher to allow it to be published for us all to share.

We should not underestimate the importance of a book such as this, for it not only reminds us (or introduces us) to a natural world full of awe and wonder, but is also a personal witness account of the inexorable decline in the biodiversity of nature over one lifetime.

I have enjoyed reading Bernard's work and I will keep referring back to it, as I intend to use it as my go to reference for sharing nature with my grand children. I think that all parents, grandparents, educators and all lovers of nature will find it an inspiring read.

The great Swedish natural scientist, Carl Linnaeus, said in 1751 - *"If you do not know the name of things, the knowledge of them is lost too."* I would humbly wish to update this quote by adding - *"If you do not know the name of things, the knowledge of them is lost too and such lack of awareness could render their extinction more acceptable"*

I encourage you to read this book and use it to nurture your love and understanding of nature - and then share it with our children.

Trevor Roach

Head of Gloucestershire Education Authority Environmental Education Service (1991 – 2002)
Head of Education and Science at the National Botanic Garden of Wales (2002 – 2008)
Friend of Bernard and Forest neighbour since 1991.

INTRODUCTION

This is a personal piece of work combining two of my loves, that of painting and the greater one, the world of nature.

My father was a practical man with a great love of and fascination with all the facets of the natural world. He passed that love on to each member of his large family.

Woodland, with its ponds and streams, was on the doorstep of our old cottage, farmland was nearby and the Severn estuary within walking distance.

Dad kept his family busy. We collected firewood from the forest, acorns and seaweed to feed our pigs and, in season, gathered blackberries, nuts, mushrooms and rosehips etc. When time permitted we liked to play in the woods with friends, building camps and exploring. We searched for birds' nests, fished and pressed wild flowers. We delighted in what nature had to offer, inevitably gaining an awareness, early in our young lives, of the profound impact it had on us. We learned to respect and appreciate its values in both practical and aesthetic terms.

Of course, as a child I did not appreciate the ingenious construction of a flower or feather, a spider's web or butterfly's wing or, indeed, a multitude of other marvels of creation. In time however, I gained a simplified understanding of the wonders of migration, pollination, metamorphosis and the interdependence of animals and plants. Gradually my childhood curiosity matured into a lifelong interest, a modest knowledge of science serving to enhance the fascination and pleasure gained from observing and engaging with our wonderful natural world.

Nature appeals to all the senses. We wonder at the bewildering diversity of animals and plants , their almost infinite forms, the variety of colour, sound and scent; the incredible resourcefulness of nature and the marvels of biological processes. All conspire to make, even the most casual engagement with natural history, immensely rewarding.

Nevertheless, I found my attempts to represent the beauty of our extraordinary natural world in paint very challenging. It was not pre-planned. Paintings were completed over a number of years, arranged chronologically and a few notes added.

The work depicts some of the personal experiences which have given me much pleasure over the years, albeit pleasure tempered with a great concern for the future state of wildlife in Britain.

Cuckoo pint and Robin

The first day of January represents a new beginning for us. It is a time to look forward to the end of winter weather and the arrival of warmer days bringing fresh new growth and the first spring migrant birds.

On the first day of January each year I look especially for the first folded rich green leaves of cuckoo pint and the tiny seedlings of cleavers pushing up from the bare earth.

During a cold winter one might have to wait a week or two for their appearance but, during relatively mild weather, some plants will have made significant growth already, for Nature doesn't pay attention to the human calendar.

Birds feeding in the snow

Hard winters bring many birds into the garden. Besides our common residents we have some welcome visitors, pied and grey wagtails, several goldfinches and siskins. A male blackcap, nuthatch and greater spotted woodpecker come occasionally, while in the hard winter of 2009/10 our most distinguished visitors were three bramblings.

It is interesting to watch birds and seek reasons for their particular feeding habits. Some species feed exclusively off the ground, others from suspended feeders and some snatch morsels of food to take away. There are birds which remain near the food source, others quickly move on.

The characters of individual birds and species are noticeable at the feeding station, the hierarchy established among blackbirds, the aggression of the robin, the defiance shown by tiny siskins and the timidity of the beautiful song thrush.

Long-tailed tits

Long-tailed tits are very active little birds. They forage in woodlands and along hedgerows in family groups keeping in touch with distinctive contact calls. These delightful little birds are always on the move and increasingly visit garden bird feeders. Invariably they remain at the feeder for a few minutes only before flying off to search for food elsewhere despite a plentiful supply of seeds and peanuts. I wonder if the reason is because insects and spiders are their main food, or could it be that their habit of keeping on the move is so compelling?

In some localities this beautiful bird was known as a bottle bird, and in another reference to its nest, the Northamptonshire poet John Clare knew it as bumbarrel. It was also known as a mumruffin or mummy-ruffin. In my local area of the Forest of Dean it was known as an 'old mon'.

Its barrel-shaped nest is indeed a wonderful piece of work. Constructed of interwoven moss, lichen, hair and cobwebs it is able to expand as the brood of up to ten grow larger. Various books state that the nest is lined with 2000 or more feathers but a friend who counted those in a ravaged nest found 400 which still seems a very large number to me.

Pheasants

When on a walk very early in January two pheasants exploded from the undergrowth in front of me. The birds' short broad stiff wings enabled them to make a rapid, though noisy, getaway. The pair had probably managed to escape from the local shoot.

Some estate owners rear pheasants and partridges in captivity maintaining woods and copses especially for them, providing extra food as necessary. These areas provide suitable habitat for many birds and animals. However, in order to maximise the pheasant poults raised, there may be, perhaps, illegal trapping and shooting of wildlife regarded as a particular threat to game birds.

Snowdrops

It is generally agreed that these beautiful flowers are not indigenous to this country although they have become naturalised in some woods.

What a welcome sight to see the hardened leaf tips pushing through frozen ground bearing the promise of spring- though it might still be far away. How lovely when they eventually flower. The sight of a large patch of snowdrops against the dark earth is quite unforgettable. One is delighted by a casual look at one of the elegant blooms; much more rewarding to push back the three pure white protective sepals for a closer examination.

I found and sketched this small group one February in what must have been the garden of an old ruined cottage; the walls had fallen down and were hidden by ivy. Yet these modest flowers must have given great pleasure to the forgotten people who once lived there.

Blue tits on an oak twig

Blue tits are among our most popular birds. They are agile, entertaining and very pretty.

I saw this pair on a bitter winter's day in oak woodland. I thought how much better they might fare if they were in a garden where they might have access to a well-stocked bird table and feeder and perhaps a box in which to roost and nest. They would be welcomed by gardeners too as they take many destructive aphids and tiny caterpillars.

In the woodland there would be meagre pickings throughout harsh winter months. As the weather warms up in the spring, insects that had been difficult to find may be more accessible, for an oak tree harbours great numbers of invertebrates.

Blue tits time their breeding cycles to coincide with the emergence of moth caterpillars. Caterpillars of the green oak tortrix moth may occur in huge numbers and can defoliate an oak tree - though the tree can produce another crop of leaves. In 1942 nest boxes were put up in local woods to provide nest sites for pied flycatchers, redstarts and tits in order to reduce the damage caused by green oak tortrix caterpillars. The boxes have been monitored since 1948.

A pair of blue tits may successfully raise six or more young in a season. Assuming the blue tit numbers remain approximately constant from year to year, many birds will die.

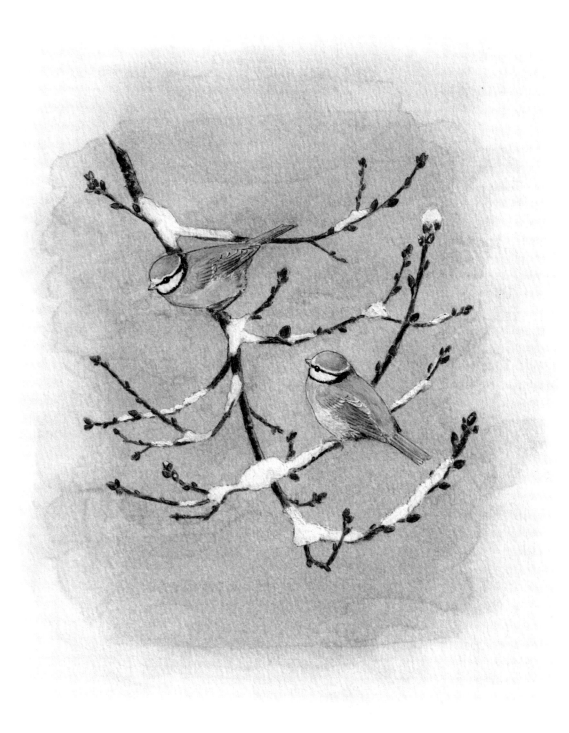

Woodmice

I placed this small bird table on top of a hawthorn hedge so that we could watch birds feeding from our kitchen window. In late afternoons during winter a pair of woodmice could often be seen making their way up through the hedge on to the table. Remaining watchful, they would feed for perhaps a minute then disappear.

Woodmice are equipped with big eyes and large mobile ears and are able to move very quickly in leaps and bounds. They have great need to be ever alert however, as they have many enemies, including owls, kestrels, stoats, weasels, foxes and cats.

Siskins and redpolls on alder

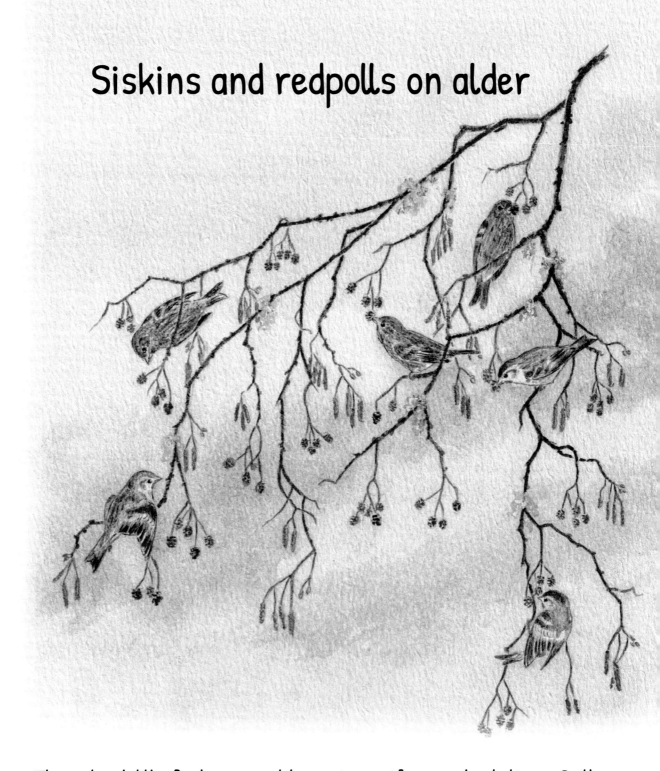

These two little finches are at home in coniferous plantations. Both are about the same size and have sharp beaks, well adapted for feeding on conifer seeds. Outside the breeding season parties of both birds can be seen feeding acrobatically together on birch and alder seeds. Both species will also take weed seeds and insects and also feed their young on insects.

During hard winters, unlike redpolls, siskins, augmented by birds from the continent, will visit bird feeders in gardens. Here they show much aggression keeping other birds, even larger ones, away from the food.

Goldfinches feeding

Goldfinches feed mainly on weed seeds but find it increasingly difficult to find enough food in winter. Our desire for tidiness has resulted in the loss of so-called waste land where wild plants were once allowed to grow to maturity. The problem is compounded by the carefree cutting of roadside verges by local councils resulting in the loss of plants which once supported many insect species, birds and small mammals.

Starlings

Starlings are common birds whose numbers are swollen in winter by birds from the continent. They are very noisy and make excellent vocal mimics, copying other birds and mechanical sounds.

Individuals behave reasonably well, but when in gangs they become the hooligans of the bird world. When a raucous band descends on a bird table the tearaways have no trouble driving all other birds away, effecting a complete takeover and bolting all the food available.

Starlings take a wide range of food. The illustration shows them prodding grassland for leatherjackets, wireworms and other invertebrates.

Before roosting starlings gather in vast flocks performing amazing

aerial displays before finally diving to roost, often in large reed beds. When roosting in cities the bickering noises they make as they settle down can be a nuisance, much worse are their droppings which foul buildings and pavements causing civic authorities to take preventative measures.

Starlings, with their sparkling iridescent plumage, are confident and brash, boisterous, swaggering and bullying. They seem to have adopted the worst of human traits, yet like them or loathe them, there is much to admire about them.

Hazel catkins

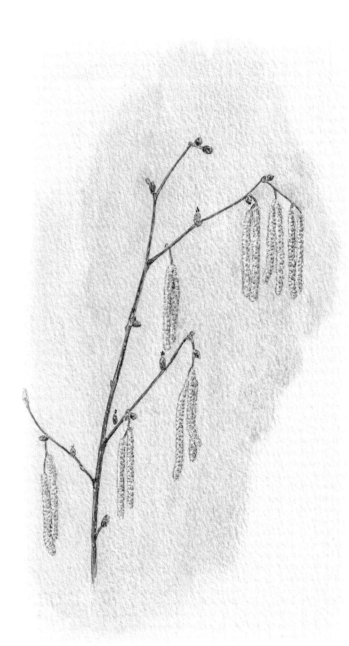

As a child in primary school our teacher would place a pot of hazel twigs on a window ledge in spring for us to see the beautiful male catkins develop. I don't think she was aware of the tiny red female flowers. They are often inconspicuous and are of course wind pollinated.

Historically, coppiced hazel was very important in the rural economy. Cleft hazel rods were used in the house building technique of wattle and daub. Today hazel rods are used in thatching, hedge laying and to make wattle hurdles. Another strange use of hazel twigs is in the mysterious art of water divining.

Robins in a territorial dispute

The robin is probably Britain's best-loved bird. In Europe it is said to be timid but here it may become quite tame, even taking mealworms out of the hand. But it doesn't extend this apparently affable nature to other birds, not even its own kind. Indeed, it can be a pugnacious little bird often driving other birds from the bird table.

Historically, the robin probably got much of its food following large animals in woodland, picking off the insects they disturbed. This tendency persists in a domestic setting as the robin searches for invertebrates around the feet of gardeners.

Robins are strongly territorial which might make finding a mate

problematic. Disputes may be resolved by the birds squaring up to each other and puffing out their red breasts. If this doesn't settle the disagreement a full-scale brawl may result which can, sometimes, lead to death.

When a suitable partner is found the male strengthens the bond by supplying the female with items of food. This also brings the female into prime condition for egg laying.

Territorial disputes could pose problems for fledglings were it not for the fact that young birds do not have the provocative red breast until they are independent.

Magpies

Magpies are interesting members of the crow family. Though they appear simply black and white, a closer look will reveal a blue-green, purple and bronze iridescence on wings and tail.

Sometimes magpies gather in much larger numbers than shown in the illustration. Such gatherings are referred to as parliaments. Two pairs met regularly over a couple of weeks in late February near the bottom of our garden. It seemed they wanted to settle an argument. There would be long quiet periods- perhaps intervals for thought, as if the birds were mulling over relevant details and issues for debate. There would then be a sudden noisy animated outburst of raucous bickering, similar in intensity to the parliament at Westminster, that sounded as if it would develop into a vicious free-for-all. Another quiet period for cogitation would follow before the next outbreak of clamorous wrangling. And so it went on - there being no physical contact. About a week later it was evident that one pair had clearly won the argument. A decision had been made, for a pair of magpies had built a large domed nest in the hawthorn where the birds had met.

Magpies are attracted to shiny and colourful objects which they carry back to their nests. These fascinating birds though are generally disliked. Besides seeds, grain, fruit and carrion, they also take eggs and nestlings of other birds and are blamed, probably unjustly, for the decline in small bird species.

Mandarin ducks

These exotic-looking ducks originated from Japan, China and Eastern Russia. Birds were released from collections in the Home Counties and are now well established in Britain. I saw this group resting on fallen branches, in a sheltered area, at the edge of a large pond in mature woodland. It was very noticeable how the extravagant colours of the mandarin drakes contrasted with the murky water.

Though the birds may get food by dabbling, they feed mainly on land taking plants, seeds, acorns, insects and snails.

Mandarins nest off the ground in tree cavities. Ducklings are encouraged to leap from the nest hole and are led to the water by the duck where they are joined by the drake who helps to protect them.

Featured in oriental art, mandarin ducks are regarded as symbols of wedded bliss and fidelity.

Frogs spawning

Once, early in March, after a refreshing shower and prior to spawning, I counted over a hundred frogs sitting motionless around our small garden pond. Each frog looked quite benign, yet en masse, appearing with a menace worthy of a horror film.

In our pond spawning takes place any time from the middle of February to late March - then the fascinating development process of the amphibians begins.

Amphibians worldwide are reported as being in severe decline; some authorities say that about one third are in danger of extinction. Sadly, in Britain, the common frog is becoming increasingly scarce also- due, partly at least, to the filling in of ponds and the use of insecticides. Garden ponds are therefore now a most important habitat for creatures that were once so common.

Our native frogs have effective cryptic colouration, while some in tropical rain forests display vivid patterns of red or yellow and black warning colours, advertising their toxicity.

Song thrush

Looking at the increasingly scarce song thrush visiting the garden one sees a wonderful example of how beautiful a superficially brown bird can be.

Some bird species rely on colour and visual cues to attract a mate and defend a territory, while others use sound. As a general rule, duller coloured species like the song thrush, warblers, and larks sing loudly and often. Brightly coloured species tend to have lesser songs or sing less frequently.

Choosing a high perch, the song thrush may sing from as early as September. It is well known that it repeats its song phrases, often several times. It accomplishes each phrase with great ease, appearing confident of exactly what it wants to say. The result is a loud, clear, unfussy and full song. In contrast, the blackbird's lovely singing tails off from time to time as if it becomes short of breath before it finishes what it wants to say.

To hear song birds in full voice is one of the great pleasures of life and, despite what a scientist might say, there are times when they appear to sing for sheer joy.

Some deciduous March twigs to identify

Buds in opposite pairs	Buds black	ash
	Buds green with brown scales, fawn twig, raised pores	elder
	Buds red brown and slender, twig slender, red, shiny	dogwood
	Large brown sticky terminal bud, twig stout, large leaf scars	horse-chestnut
	Buds green with brown edges, stout twig with prominent leaf scars	sycamore
	Buds green with brown edges, on a slender green twig	spindle
Buds alternate	Buds green, twig greenish brown	hazel
	Buds red plump and shiny, twig reddish	lime
	Buds dull purple, twig dark with raised pores	alder
	Buds dull mid brown clustered at end of stout twig	oak
	Small dark brown buds, twigs very thin, dark brown and shiny	birch
	Buds with whitish down and dark brown scales, twig fawn with large pale pores	rowan
	Smallish pale brown buds on white twig	white poplar
	Shiny pale buds very close to yellow twig	crack willow
	Pale brown buds, slim and sharply pointed	beech

The rookery

Rooks are members of the crow family. They are about the same size as carrion crows but the adults have bare face patches and thickly feathered thighs. Rooks are associated with farmland and, unlike crows, are communal birds.

Flocks may be seen in fields feeding together with jackdaws on grain but compensate for this undesirable trait by probing the soil for agricultural pests such as slugs, snails, grubs, beetles, leather jackets and wire-worms.

Rooks nest colonially in rookeries. In early spring they are busy making good the damage done by winter storms to their old nests before the trees come into leaf. Rooks are said to nest 'socially'. If that means harmoniously it was certainly not the case with the largest rookery that I was familiar with in my youth. It comprised about 200 nests in trees near the banks of the river Severn. There was incessant loud, harsh cawing but there were squabbles too for rooks are not averse to stealing twigs from unattended nests rather than searching for their own building materials. Then the clamour would increase. A terrific commotion would result which somehow settled differences and eventually the tumult would subside. Often, besides egg shells, whole eggs and naked young could be found beneath the trees as a result of such a fracas. Perhaps one might expect a certain amount of criminal behaviour where space and food resources are at a premium. Such conduct reflects certain aspects of human life in the chronically overcrowded slum areas of big cities that Charles Dickens knew, for these were also known as 'rookeries'.

Nonetheless, the sounds produced by a busy rookery are a pleasure to hear and so evocative of the cherished rural Britain I knew as a boy.

Alder twig

The picture shows the pollen producing male catkins together with the tiny female catkins and leaf buds of a typical alder twig in early spring. Also shown are the cone-like remains of the fruit. After pollination the female catkins develop into spherical green fruits. When they mature they become woody and during the winter open out to release numerous winged seeds relished by redpolls and siskins.

Like bog myrtle and sea buckthorn, alder has root nodules containing bacteria which enable it to 'fix' nitrogen from the air, similar to plants of the pea family.

Alder grows best on wet ground and stabilises the banks of streams. The wood is reddish and was used to make clogs.

Cuckoo pint

By March, cuckoo pint plants that were bursting through the soil in early January, will have made luxuriant growth due to the substantial tuberous rootstock.

The botanic name of the plant is *Arum maculatum*; maculatum means spotted. Looking at cuckoo pint plants in my local area over several weeks in the spring of 2011, I found that of 1000 plants just 95 had spotted leaves, a percentage of 9.5. The amount of spotting on the leaves varied a great deal and one plant in particular was almost completely covered with dark blotches.

Much folklore is attached to cuckoo pint. Some authorities say there are more than 70 local names for the plant.

Fallow deer

Most illustrations of fallow deer show the pale brown spotted animals of parkland. However, there are several colour variations from dark brown to white. Those in our local woods in the Forest of Dean are a mid-brown colour with no obvious spots.

The best time to catch a glimpse of them is at dawn or dusk during the winter when there are few leaves on the trees to hide them.

Widgeon

On one of my regular trips to the banks of the Severn estuary in early March I heard the musical whistling of what could only be a drake widgeon. Then I spotted it with others. Two pairs were poking casually through some bladderwrack on the muddy banks. The birds had probably strayed from Slimbridge Widllife Trust a few miles up the river.

My previous experience of widgeon has been seeing flocks of about forty grazing like geese on grassland.

Widgeon are winter visitors from Scandinavia and Russia, though some are said to nest in Scotland.

Common Garden Snail Shells

Roman Snail

Black-Lipped Banded Snail Shells

White-Lipped Banded Snail Shells

Crystal Snail

Great Pond Snail

Ramshorn Snail

Snail shells

Snails belong to the class of molluscs known as gastropods; it includes slugs, limpets and whelks. Illustrated are the shells of several species of snails which I found in my garden after a brief search. Clusters of the common garden snail were located in a number of sheltered places in crevices and flower pots. Snails have strong homing instincts and each snail has both male and female sex organs. They are nocturnal, avoiding desiccating sunshine, and need to eat food rich in calcium - vital for shell construction.

A snail prepares for hibernation by first finding a safe frost-free hideaway. It then withdraws completely into its shell, secreting a slimy material over the opening. This dries forming an effective hard seal.

I couldn't resist painting the shell of the common garden snail from different angles. Compare its size to that of the Roman snails. It is our largest snail and is eaten as escargot. I found this shell on the Cotswold Hills, a limestone area.

Many black-lipped and white-lipped banded snails were found in my garden, white-lipped sorts outnumbering the black-lipped by about five to two. I found huge variations in the appearance of both types. Both normally have up to five dark bands which may be fused together.

Snails living in light places tend to be light while those inhabiting dark shady spots are darker in colour.

Several small glassy shells of the crystal snail were also found in the garden but the two pond snail shells were from a woodland pond.

The wren

This beautiful little bird can be found in a wide variety of habitats including gardens, copses, woodland and heath. Its flight is fast and direct.

It searches low down in dense vegetation, like a little feathered mouse, probing into crevices, picking up insects, spiders and small seeds with its slender bill. The wren is very active, always on the move except when it explodes into song. The song itself is a rapid outburst of penetrating rattling notes, unbelievably loud for such a small bird, its tiny body vibrating with the effort. It is delivered with such an intensity that ensures its presence is known.

Locally the wren was known as the 'fern owl' due to the fact that it uses dry bracken to construct its nest, in our area at least. The male builds several nests for females to choose from. The selected nest is lined with soft material and up to about eight eggs laid. Wrens may produce two broods a year.

The wren is one of our commonest birds but being tiny, its numbers can be severely depleted in harsh weather. To cope with winter cold, several birds may shelter together in a confined space, perhaps a nest box, where they share the generated warmth. Fortunately, due to its ability to produce many young, wren numbers can quickly recover.

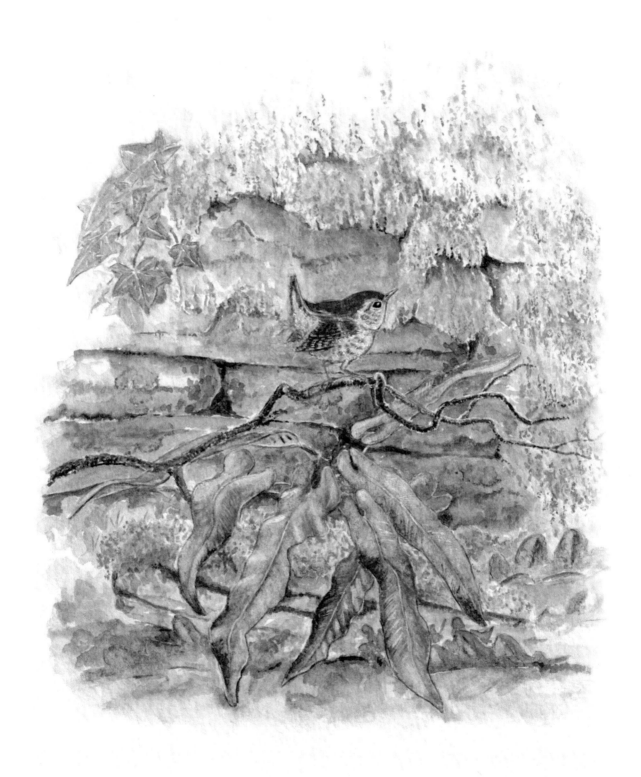

Blackthorn

The scientific name of blackthorn is *Prunus spinosa*, meaning 'spiny plum'. This small tree suckers readily, making very dense and thorny thickets and hedges, favoured as nesting sites by many birds. It may flower as early as March, often before it comes into leaf, when it is visited by numerous insects, especially moths.

A bad spell of weather, that

often coincides with blackthorn flowering, is popularly known as a 'blackthorn winter'. The fruits are the familiar bitter sloes which can be made into wine and may be used to flavour gin. The wood is hard and used to make walking sticks and also, traditionally, the Irish shillelagh.

Hybrid larch

Larch is unusual among coniferous trees because it is deciduous, losing its golden coloured needles in autumn. In spring, just after the flowers form, tufts of fresh, bright green needles are produced on very short stubby spurs.

The female flowers are much more conspicuous, being erect and a beautiful delicate pink.

Foresters prefer Japanese and hybrid larches to the European larch as they grow more vigorously.

Conifers, such as larch, spruce, pine and Douglas fir etc. are of great economic importance providing timber for construction work, crates, telegraph poles, plywood, fences, block floors and so on.

The sighing of the wind in a conifer plantation contrasts with the leafy fluttering it generates in an oak or beech wood.

Snake's head fritillary

The snake's head fritillary is a rare native bulbous plant of wet meadows. The purplish petals have a unique chequered pattern which is one of the reasons for its appeal to gardeners.

Some people consider this beautiful plant easy to grow but my attempts with seeds and bulbs have been disappointing. The unopened flower is supposed to look like a snake's head. Its name is from 'fritillus' meaning dice box.

Tufted ducks

The mallard is a dabbling duck, feeding mostly from the surface of ponds, lakes and slow rivers, while the tufted duck is a diver. Diving ducks tend to sit deeper in the water than surface feeders. Their legs too are set further back on their bodies making them adept at swimming under water but relatively clumsy when moving on land.

Tufted ducks dive for fresh water molluscs, small fish, insects and water plants preferring deeper water than mallards.

The female tufted duck has the cryptic colouring of a ground nesting bird in contrast to the striking black and white livery of the drake.

In my youth these beautiful birds were a rarity but are now quite often seen on local ponds and lakes.

Wild daffodils

The wild daffodil has been adopted as the national flower of Wales and also the county flower of Gloucestershire. Daffodils belong to the same family as snowdrops and share the same sort of habitat, flowering about a month later. They are principally plants of damp woods but in March and April can bloom prolifically on grassland. Indeed they grow in such profusion on the Gloucestershire Herefordshire border that in the 1930's the Great Western Railway Company ran 'Daffodil Specials' from London to one particular corner of Gloucestershire enabling people to enjoy the glorious sight of whole woods and fields carpeted with these enchanting flowers.

The central brightly coloured trumpet is surrounded by paler petals giving the blooms a most attractive modest beauty in contrast to the larger gaudy garden forms. Daffodil seeds take six or seven years to develop into flowering plants.

Sadly, again the story is one of decline. The number of wild daffodils has been seriously reduced due to loss of habitat, more land having been brought into cultivation. The problem has been compounded by the misguided planting of garden types in close proximity to our wild daffodils, while some local authorities plant roadside verges with cheap, readily available, bulbs. This is of great concern to botanists for daffodils hybridise freely and may result in the loss of our true native species – *Narcissuss pseudonarcisuss*.

Feral boar family

From the top of an old slag heap I watched this family of boar through binoculars. Just having fed, they were in a relaxed mood. While the sow lay stretched out, no doubt enjoying a welcome but sleepless rest, the youngsters, known locally as humbugs, were rooting around contentedly. They were quietly picking up titbits of food and exploring their surroundings as any youngsters would. Piglets are the most endearing of young animals and quite fascinating to watch.

The boar in the Forest of Dean are feral, having originated from escapees from farms or were deliberately released. There are mixed views as to their desirability in the area. While it may be pleasant to see a group of these animals - known as a sunder- in the woodlands, they have been causing a considerable amount of costly damage to roadside verges, open areas, recreational spaces and sports grounds. The authorities are working towards an optimum number that the Forest can sustain.

Wayside flowers

I saw this little group of flowers growing together on a steep hedge bank.

The odd primrose and lesser celandine may appear as early as January, though it is not until March that spring flowers make a proper show.

The primroses illustrated are the pin-eyed sort, each having a prominent visible pistil and concealed stamens. Thrum-eyed primroses have the reverse arrangement. The two flower types are never found on the same plant.

Lesser celandines are members of the buttercup family. Their glossy golden colour contrast wth the pale modesty of primroses. The contrast is reflected in the leaves too, each appearing perfectly suited to its flower.

The abundance of dog violets varies from year to year in my local area as does the ratio of white to purple blooms. The term 'dog" also used for dog rose, refers to a perceived inferiority in some way. Dog violets, having no scent, are regarded as inferior to highly fragrant sweet violets.

The tiny white flowers illustrated are those of barren strawberries. Wide gaps between its petals distinguish it from the wild strawberries which bear such delicious fruits.

Historically, the banks of lanes and narrow roads have been a rich source of wild flowers. Sadly, it is noticeable that, in recent years, many such banks have been cut up by larger tractors and farm machinery resulting in a reduction of our beautiful wayside flora.

Willow warbler or Chiffchaff?

The willow warbler and chiffchaff are very similar, both in appearance and the habitat they occupy. There are subtle differences but their songs are unmistakable and something to look forward to in early spring.

The chiffchaff's cheerful repetitive 'chiffchaff' appears to be a confident assertion that the bright days of spring will go on forever. In contrast, the willow warbler's fluent, wistful song of descending notes, evoke feelings of regret that the wonderful days of spring are finite and would soon be over.

The bird illustrated is likely to be a chiffchaff as it is much more common in our area than the willow warbler. Furthermore, sometimes the male pussy willow has finished flowering before the later arrival from Africa of the willow warbler as was the case when I drew this picture.

Wood anemones

Like bluebells, wood sorrel and dog's mercury, wood anemones are flowers of ancient woodland. These pretty flowers present an enchanting display in spring as they carpet the floor of ancient woods. They are at their best on a sunny day before the trees come into leaf. If the weather is dull or wet, the flowers close and droop, thus protecting their pollen. They are members of the buttercup family and poisonous.

What appears to be petals are regarded as sepals by botanists; usually there are six but sometimes as many as nine. They are white, often tinged with pink, especially on the undersides.

It was thought that the anemone turned away from even the slightest breeze hence its popular alternative name of windflower, the Greek word for wind being 'anemos'.

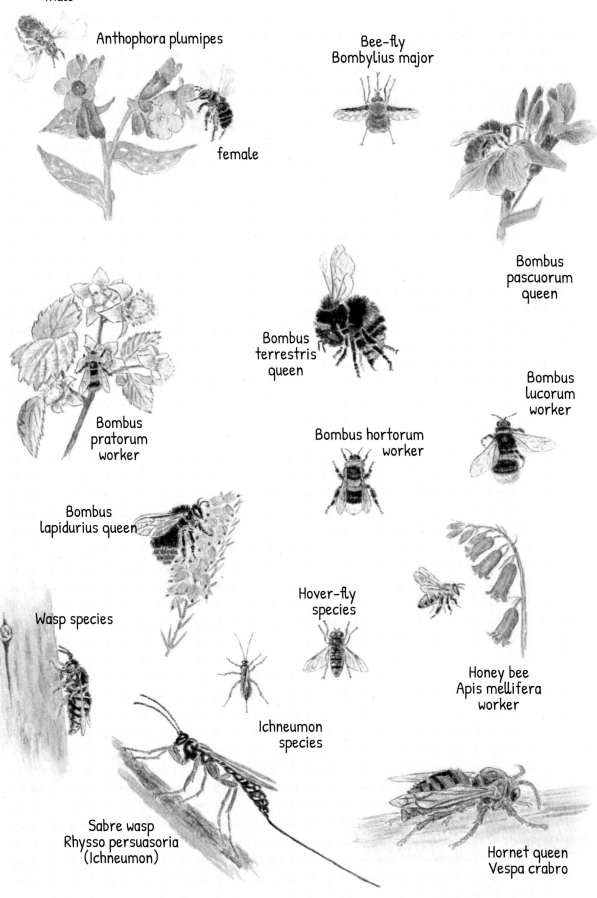

male

Anthophora plumipes

female

Bee-fly
Bombylius major

Bombus
pascuorum
queen

Bombus
terrestris
queen

Bombus
pratorum
worker

Bombus
lucorum
worker

Bombus hortorum
worker

Bombus
lapidurius queen

Wasp species

Hover-fly
species

Honey bee
Apis mellifera
worker

Ichneumon
species

Sabre wasp
Rhysso persuasoria
(Ichneumon)

Hornet queen
Vespa crabro

Mostly Bees

The order Hymenoptera includes bees, wasps and ichneumon flies. Most bee and wasp species are solitary insects. Those illustrated, except for *Anthophora plumipes*, are social insects and live in colonies. Many wasp species are parasitic.

When watching *anthophora plumipes* on pulmonaria I noticed they only visited pink flowers as opposed to the older blue flowers.

Bees, especially honey bees, are insects of enormous economic importance as pollinators of many food plants. Honey bees are active from early spring to late autumn. I saw one visiting heather in a garden centre on a bright sunny day in 2013 as early as January 9th.

Honey bees construct hexagonal cells on vertical cones, using wax secreted from glands on the abdomen. Wasps use chewed wood to make horizontal combs. Wasps are able to sting several times, but bees have barbed stings which detach, remaining in the victim's flesh, but resulting in the death of the bee.

While working in my shed, in early spring, I found a hornet at the window, its low drone quite unlike the aggressive sound of a wasp. It must have been a queen that found my shed a desirable place to hibernate.

Ichneumon flies are solitary insects. They make up a large group of parasitic insects whose larvae live in, or on, other insect larvae. I once watched the impressive sabre wasp on a pine log. Incredibly, it can detect a larva in the wood and drill down to lay an egg on it.

The bee-fly and hover-fly, having just one pair of wings, belong to the order Diptera. Both are mimics. The bee-fly appears superficially like a bumblebee and can be seen visiting primroses when its long proboscis is easily seen. With their black and yellow warning colours, hover-flies are considered to be wasp mimics, but look much more benign to me.

The swallow

Alerted by its distinctive cheerful twittering, as if the bird is expressing joy at being close to journey's end, I usually see my first swallow of the year very early in April. Always, it seems, it is a single bird flying purposefully in a northerly direction. But, 'one swallow doesn't make a summer', the main body arrives a little later. Not only are these delightful birds harbingers of summer they are its very essence.

I love to see swallows in high summer in a field of cattle, the animals disturbing insects in the grass, obliging the birds to exercise their remarkable flying skills twisting and turning at high speed to snap up a meal in full flight; the ultimate in fast food.

Setting out in February, swallows navigate from South Africa, a journey of about 6000 miles, fraught with dangers of many kinds. It is, of course, just another of Nature's marvels.

Ivy in April

The non-flowering stems of ivy climb by means of aerial roots and bear the familiar three and five - lobed leaves. Simple leaves, without lobes, grow on the bushy flowering branches. The fruit is usually ripe by December and may remain as late as April providing a wonderful winter food resource for blackbirds, thrushes and pigeons.

Crab apple blossom

The crab apple twig illustrated, was from a lone tree about five metres high growing in a wood of immature oak trees.

The fruit is small, bitter and hard, but despite its bitterness crab apples are made into jellies, jam and cider. The humble crab apple is the ancestor of all the well known cultivated varieties. Its root stock is still used on which new apple varieties are grafted.

Apple blossom is always beautiful, that of the crab no less so. Horticulturists have developed varieties with showy flowers, colourful autumn leaves and fruit as small decorative garden trees.

Jackdaws at their des res

The jackdaw is one of the smallest members of the crow family and arguably the one with the most defined character. What it lacks in size it makes up for with its blustering, haughty manner. Watch a jackdaw in the breeding season and you will see an arrogant, strutting show off. Jackdaws are habitual thieves too - but I like them.

This pair seemed proud of their chosen nest site but whether they successfully reared young there I do not know.

Grey wagtails

All wagtails are delightful little birds but perhaps the grey wagtail is the most beautiful. It is a bird of tumbling mountain streams and woodland brooks; it seems to delight in splashing water. It can be seen perched on a stone, or the low branch of an alder, flicking its tail continuously. Grey wagtails share the same sort of habitat where one might encounter a dipper bobbing up and down searching for food.

Whereas the dipper finds food from a bed of a stream or river - even walking under water- the grey wagtail may be seen to leap into the air, in a short dancing flight, to snap up a passing fly. Like other wagtails it is insectivorous taking damsel flies, mayflies, beetles and midges also snails and freshwater shrimps from shallow water. Its long tail, longer than those of other wagtails, enables the bird to change direction rapidly in mid air, skilfully contriving to catch insects on the wing.

The birds illustrated were making their way up a woodland stream with frequent stops for food. They moved off with an exaggerated bouncy undulating flight keeping in touch with distinctive contact calls.

The moorhen

The moorhen is a delightful bird of ponds, lakes, slow moving streams and rivers, its strange guttural call echoing across the water. It is interesting to watch, for as it swims its head jerks. When walking it flicks its tail.

Moorhens feed on fruit, seeds, waterweeds, worms, slugs, snails and other invertebrates.

Their feet are not webbed, but they have long flattened toes, fine for walking on mud or submerged vegetation, but not ideal for swimming.

I once startled a moorhen that was swimming near the bank of a narrow river. It dived and remained totally out of sight submerged amongst the tangled roots of an alder. It stayed under water for several minutes, reappearing when I moved away.

As a boy I knew a small pond where, in season, I was sure to see a moorhen's nest with its beautiful spotted eggs. Alas, there are no birds there now - nor is there a pond.

Male kestrel

The adaptable kestrel is found on farmland, sea cliffs and in urban areas, and is often seen over motorway verges. It hunts by hovering, hence its alternative name of windhover. It flies into the wind at the same rate as the wind is blowing it back. As it faces into the wind it flaps its wings vigorously while keeping its head perfectly still. It is said that kestrels can detect ultra-violet light which enables them to locate voles because they leave a trail of urine wherever they go and their urine glows in ultra-violet light. Kestrels will take mice, also small birds, worms, insects and other invertebrates.

The bird shown is a male; the female is brown with a barred tail.

A mixed border

Providing suitable conditions prevail, with plenty of light, a certain amount of shelter, sufficient moisture and acceptable soil, the hedge banks bordering a country lane can be a wonderful source of wildlife, especially wild flowers. The specific conditions of a habitat will determine what species will thrive in it.

Various plant families will be represented with differing flower colours and forms. Plants with weaker stems will be supported by those with rigid stalks while short species tolerate the shade cast by taller kinds. There will be a variety of leaf shapes too, all producing food for the plants from carbon dioxide and water using the energy of sunlight, a process known as photosynthesis.

The sight of such a hedge bank is one of the great joys of springtime.

The wild flowers illustrated are some of those one might see in May, they include:-

Hawthorn, in the background.

Red campion

Garlic mustard or jack-by-the-hedge

Common vetch

Bluebell

Yellow archangel

Herb Robert

Also shown is black bryony climbing bracken

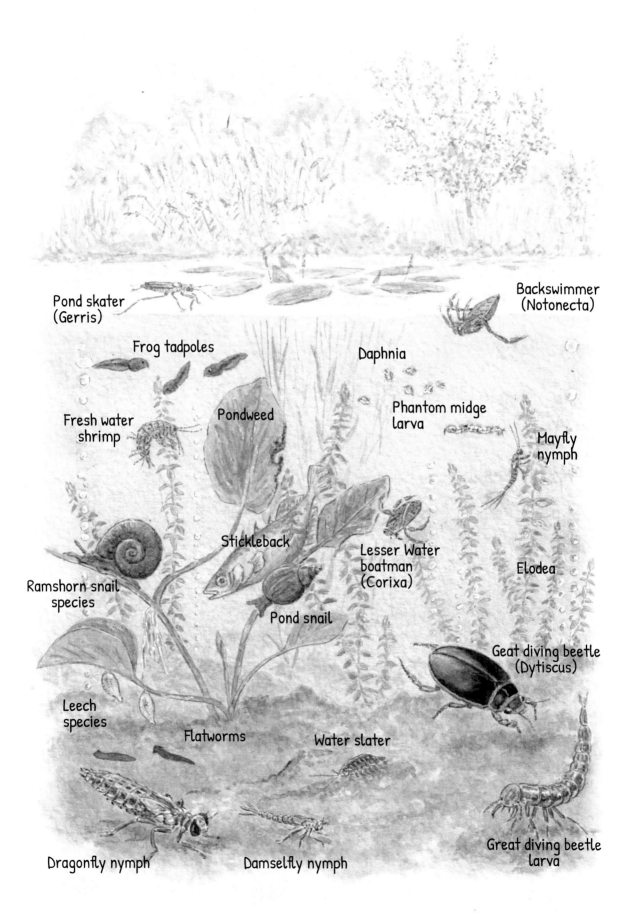

Pond skater
(Gerris)

Backswimmer
(Notonecta)

Frog tadpoles

Daphnia

Fresh water
shrimp

Pondweed

Phantom midge
larva

Mayfly
nymph

Ramshorn snail
species

Stickleback

Lesser Water
boatman
(Corixa)

Elodea

Pond snail

Geat diving beetle
(Dytiscus)

Leech
species

Flatworms

Water slater

Dragonfly nymph

Damselfly nymph

Great diving beetle
larva

Pond animals

A pond in an open area, not shaded by vegetation can provide the ideal habitat for a host of aquatic species. A woodland pond with the bottom choked with leaves will have low oxygen levels and consequently little life. The depth is important too, for some species may be unable to tolerate the wide temperature ranges of shallow water. A healthy pond consists of a balanced community of interdependent animals and plants. Microscopic green organisms are consumed by daphnia and grazed by herbivores like snails. Nourishment is thus provided for carnivorous animals and a food chain established - in reality a complex food web results.

Representative animals from five different groups or phyla are shown: Platyhelminthes - flat worms, Annelids - leeches, Molluscs - snails, Chordates - stickleback, and the largest group in any pond - the Arthropods. Arthropods are invertebrates with jointed limbs and include insects and crustaceans. What are not shown are the microscopic organisms at the base of the food chain that break down organic materials into simple substances that can be used again by plants.

Pond animals display great diversity of form and mode of life. Adult mayflies, dragonflies and damselflies fly of course, but so can water boatmen, diving beetles, pond skaters and midges. Snails, shrimps, flatworms are confined to the pond unless they can escape on the feet of birds, perhaps as eggs. Most pond animals use gills to obtain oxygen from the water. The diving beetle larva takes air from the water surface through tail appendages while the adult stores air beneath its wing cases. Freshwater shrimps require water with high oxygen levels, unlike pond slaters, feeding on detritus at the bottom of the pond, they can tolerate low oxygen levels.

The blackbird

The blackbird is very well known for its rich warbling song. When startled it produces a rapid outburst of loud chattering notes, and utters a loud persistent 'pink, pink, pink' alarm when it perceives a threat, perhaps the sight of a prowling cat. Often this continues at dusk, for what seems, no apparent reason. One fears it might betray the bird's location to potential predators.

A pair of blackbirds were raising young in a nest they had built in our hedge. Plenty of earthworms were available in our garden and the birds took full advantage. The male regularly perched on a wooden trellis momentarily, before delivering his beakful of worms to the clamouring nestlings. During that time, even though his beak was closed around the worms, he sang quite loudly.

Young birds need a diet with sufficient protein-rich food to sustain their high growth rate. Blackbirds eat a similar range of food to its close relative the song thrush, but consumes a much higher proportion of fruit. The thrush prefers animal matter, slugs, snails and other invertebrates.

Minibeasts

The small animals illustrated overleaf represent a tiny fraction of the many species that can be found in Britain. Most of those shown were found in my small garden.

Whether these small creatures have six, eight, fourteen, or many more legs, or none at all, whether they are carnivores, herbivores, have hard exteriors or soft, whether they are quick or slow, run, leap, fly or just wriggle, each fills its own particular niche in the rich web of life. Each has its own defence strategy. It may be displaying warning colours, exuding distasteful fluids, mimicking aggressive species, biting or stinging, running quickly into loose soil or leaf litter, feigning death or simply flying away.

Though most small creatures are considered benign, some are regarded as pests and others allies. In my garden the larvae of vine weevils are troublesome as they eat the roots of pot plants. The damage caused by slugs also, especially small ones, can be extensive. Looking like bird droppings, the mess left by lily beetles must be seen to be believed, each disgusting blob concealing a larva. Agriculture has its own war to wage on pests.

Earthworms, of course, are friends of gardeners by aerating the soil and increasing its fertility by pulling organic debris into the soil. The adults and larvae of green lacewings and ladybirds eat aphids which, in large numbers, can cause so much damage by sucking the sap of choice plants, while bees perform the economically important task of pollinating many crops.

Few can fail to marvel at the amazing aerial skills of a dragonfly or wonder how a spider avoids being trapped in one of its own incredible snares.

The small animals we share the earth with are all truly fascinating.

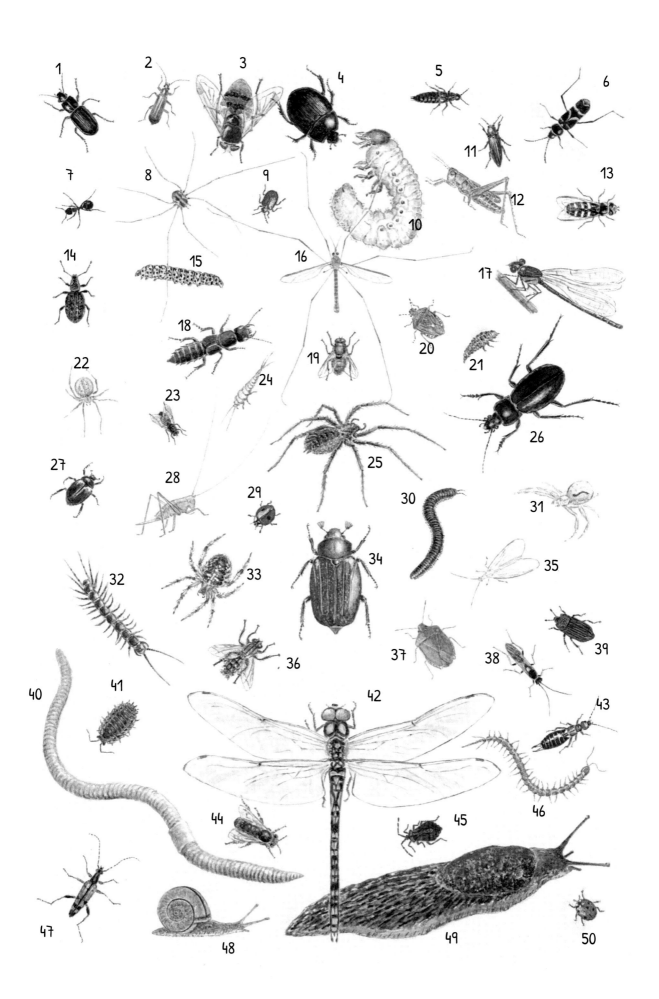

Identification list of the small animals illustrated

1. ground beetle
2. soldier beetle
3. hover-fly
4. dor beetle
5. rove beetle
6. wasp beetle
7. wood ant
8. harvestman
9. lily beetle
10. cockchafer larva
11. click beetle
12. meadow grasshopper
13. hover-fly
14. vine weevil
15. mullien moth caterpillar
16. crane fly
17. large red damselfly
18. devil's coach horse
19. green bottle
20. sloe bug
21. ladybird larva
22. unidentified spider
23. house fly
24. silverfish
25. house spider
26. violet ground beetle
27. garden chafer
28. bush cricket
29. two spot ladybird
30. black snake millipede
31. crab spider
32. centipede
33. cross spider
34. cockchafer
35. green lacewing
36. flesh fly
37. green shield bug
38. ichneumon fly
39. burying beetle
40. earthworm
41. woodlouse
42. dragonfly
43. earwig
44. honey bee
45. heath assassin bug
46. centipede
47. longhorn beetle
48. white-lipped banded snail
49. red slug
50. seven spot ladybird

I thought it would be an interesting exercise to paint some spring flowers looking directly into them

1. primrose
2. greater stitchwort
3. broad-leaved willow herb
4. wallflower
5. lesser celandine
6. wood sorrel
7. ragged robin
8. germander speedwell
9. scarlet pimpernel
10. yellow archangel
11. bird's-foot trefoil
12. dog rose
13. ramsons
14. dandelion
15. common speedwell
16. wood anemone
17. daisy
18. wild strawberry
19. dog violet
20. bugle
21. herb paris
22. bulbous buttercup

23. white campion
24. yellow pimpernel
25. coltsfoot
26. marsh marigold
27. red campion
28. lady's smock
29. cowslip
30. crab apple
31. herb Robert
32. lesser periwinkle
33. herb bennet
34. wood forgetmenot
35. oxford ragwood
36. green alkanet
37. lungwort
38. three-cornered leek
39. horse chestnut
40. hedge groundwort
41. wood spurge
42. hawthorn
43. bluebell
44. Welsh poppy

Swifts

Swifts arrive in Britain in May and stay just a few months until August. They are the last of the spring visitors to arrive and about the first to leave. I welcome these enigmatic birds and find it uplifting to see bands of them, their wings appearing to flicker, as they chase at high speed over the roof tops-screaming all the while. Swifts spend more time in the air than any other bird. Experts tell us that they catch nesting materials, sleep and even mate on the wing. Swifts feed entirely on flying insects which are funnelled into the wide gapes of their mouths aided by the surrounding stiff bristles. These insects, which might include spiderlings floating in the air, accumulate in the throat being stuck together with saliva to form a nutritious bolus to feed the nestlings. If there is a shortage of food young birds are able to achieve a state of torpor by lowering their body temperature and metabolic rate.

Extravagant claims have been made about the speed that swifts achieve and truly they must be one of the fastest birds in level flight. Again, it has been stated that a swift may fly up to 650 miles in a day when feeding growing nestlings. Undoubtedly such an aerial bird covers enormous distances but this figure can only be an estimate and impossible to substantiate.

I once found a swift grounded. It was completely helpless, but once tossed into the air, its own element, it dashed away at an impressive rate.

Sadly numbers of swifts are reported by the RSPB to have declined significantly over recent years. This is thought to be due to the loss of suitable nesting sites that older buildings provided, modern building techniques and the increasing use of insecticides.

Cowslip time

The small area of my front garden reserved for wild flowers is yellow with cowslips and yellow rattle in May. These are followed by ox-eye daisies, buttercups, hawkweed, cat's ear, and trefoils. About 30 species, which most people regard as weeds, have been identified. In some years a colony of beautiful bee orchids appears. Grasses are rendered less vigorous, for the semi-parasitic yellow rattle taps into their root systems for nutrients.

Such rich areas of wild flowers support many invertebrate species providing a vital link in the food chain.

Marsh marigold

The marsh marigold is a most imposing plant. Emerging from its thick rootstock in spring it makes rapid and luxuriant growth. The flowers are very impressive seen en masse and, in a very short time, can transform the appearance of wet meadows into a beautiful scene of green and gold.

Botanically, the flower has no petals but displays five large bright golden sepals.

This gorgeous flower has many local names including may-blob, mary bud, mollyblobs and kingcups.

The skylark

Smaller than a starling and slightly larger than a chaffinch, the skylark is an iconic little bird. The reason for its elevated status is its glorious song. It sustains its exhilarating warbling for five minutes or more as it ascends into the air, hovering almost out of sight, and continues to sing as it descends. Once common and widely distributed the joyful song of the male could be heard over sand dunes, golf courses, commons and farmland. It is a favourite of poets and musicians, inspiring Vaughan Williams to compose the wonderfully evocative 'The Lark Ascending'.

It is a ground nesting bird where its striated brown plumage affords it effective camouflage, its eggs too are mottled. It feeds largely on weed seeds, grain, insects and other small invertebrates. The skylark tends to avoid trees and hedges, feeding and nesting well away from them, thus any uncultivated field margins are of limited benefit to it.

The Royal Society for the Protection of Birds, the British trust for Ornithology and County Wildlife Trusts agree that numbers have fallen very steeply since the 1970's. This confirms my own casual observations as the bird has not been heard in the local area in recent years. The skylark is now on the RSPB Red List of 'Birds of Conservation Concern'. It appears that the days when its glorious uplifting song could be heard over almost every field is gone forever – and that diminishes all of us.

Cuckoo flower

The cuckoo flower blooms at a time when one hopes to hear the cuckoo calling. The flower is also known as milkmaids or, more popularly, lady's smock. Locally it was called pee-the-beds for it grows in damp meadowland and near streams.

Its leaves are pinnate. Leaflets high on the stalk are very narrow while those at the base are rounded, forming a rosette. The cuckoo flower is a member of the cabbage family and closely related to watercress, indeed it makes a reasonable substitute for watercress.

Break a lower leaf off and it roots readily to form a new plant.

Feathers

My young daughter made a collection of feathers and grew to realise what incredible structures they were. They were easy to identify as most feathers came from birds we found dead.

There are two main types, downy insulating feathers and flight and contour feathers. The latter sorts are illustrated.

Feathers may have modifications for a secondary purpose. One might consider, for instance, the iridescent speculum of the mallard drake or the long colourful tail feathers of the cock pheasant in attracting a mate. As a part of its courtship display the snipe dives through the air with its tail outspread. The two outer tail feathers vibrate rapidly as the air rushes over them producing a unique mechanical bleating sound known as drumming.

The stiff blade-like flight feathers of the wood pigeon, enabling it to fly rapidly, if noisily, can be compared with the soft velvety texture of an owl's wing feathers where silent flight is paramount. The stiff tail feathers of woodpeckers act as a prop and the broad vanes of a buzzard's flight feathers maximise the use of rising air currents when the bird is soaring.

At the same time concealment is vital for birds that spend a great deal of time on the ground, hence the cryptic colouring of snipe and grouse. Furthermore, female ducks and pheasants, being much less colourful than the males, are not so likely to be spotted by predators when incubating eggs.

As feathers are so important it is vital that birds keep them in good condition. This is achieved by bathing, preening, oiling and dusting, and feathers are regularly replaced by the moulting process.

Feathers are indeed wonderful, natural, multipurpose devices.

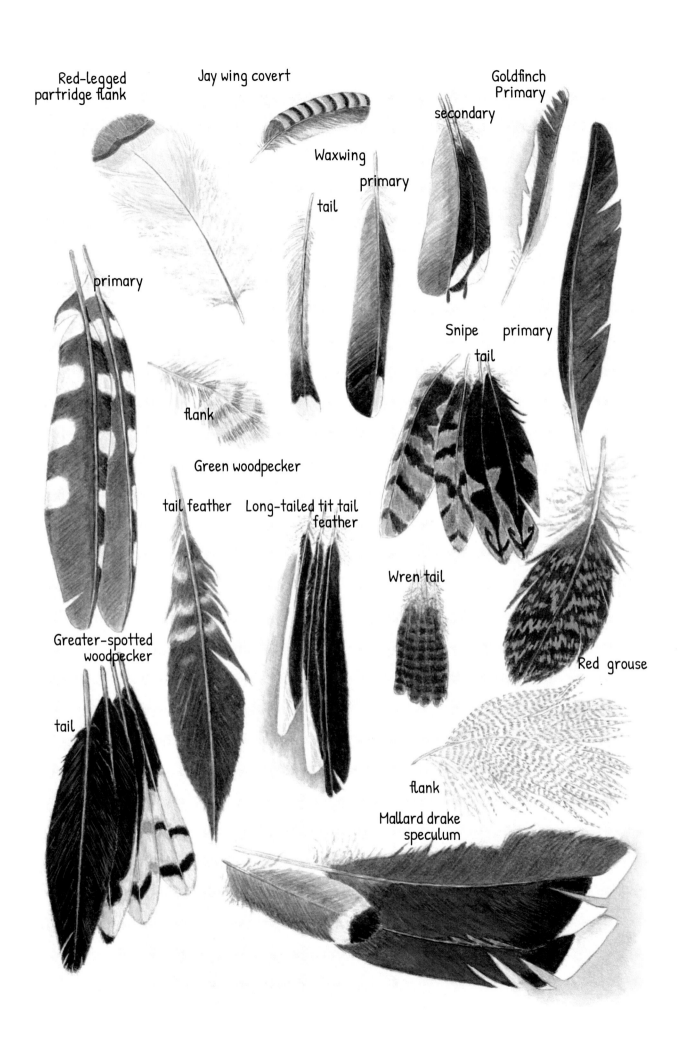

Red-legged
partridge flank

Jay wing covert

Goldfinch
Primary

secondary

Waxwing

primary

tail

primary

Snipe   primary

tail

flank

Green woodpecker

tail feather   Long-tailed tit tail
feather

Wren tail

Greater-spotted
woodpecker

Red grouse

tail

flank

Mallard drake
speculum

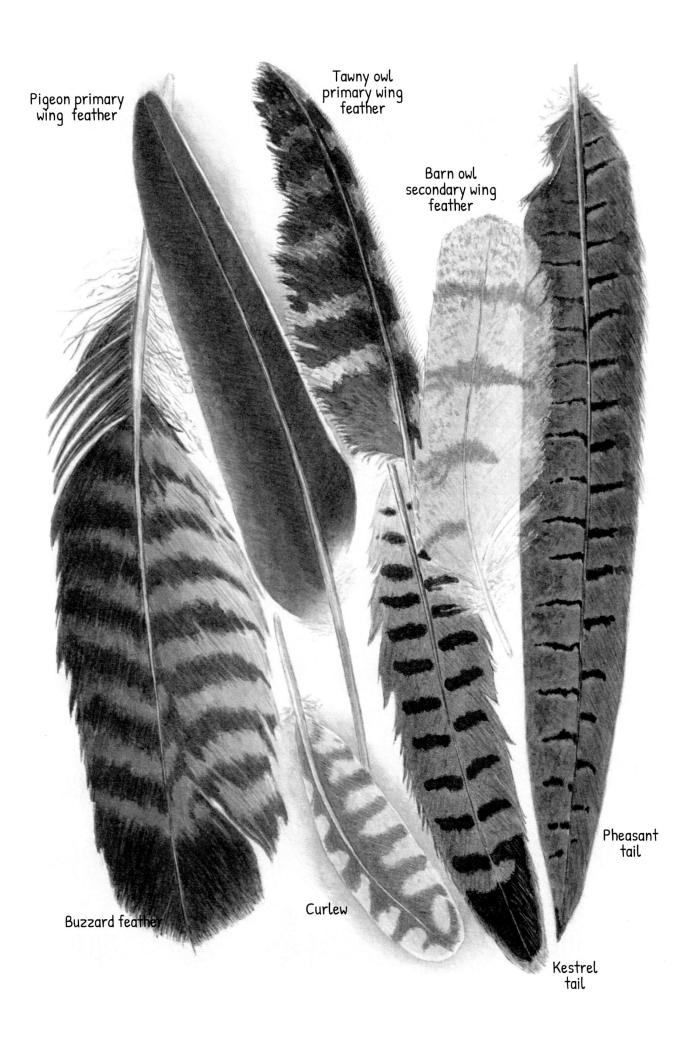

Pigeon primary wing feather

Tawny owl primary wing feather

Barn owl secondary wing feather

Buzzard feather

Curlew

Pheasant tail

Kestrel tail

83

Shelducks

Shelducks are the largest members of the duck tribe found in Britain. Both sexes have similar colouring, the drake being identified by the large red knob at the base of its beak. With its large size, and relatively long neck, the shelduck appears goose-like, perhaps it is an intermediate form between ducks and geese. Geese are more aggressive than ducks. They have shorter beaks, ideal for picking up grain and cropping short grass. Ducks, in general, including shelducks, take more animal matter, insects, molluscs and crustaceans.

Shelducks nest in a hidden spot, sometimes a rabbit burrow, so the duck has no need of the cryptic plumage of most other duck species.

The pair of ducks illustrated were seen many times on the muddy banks of the Severn estuary.

Once, as children, we found a pretty little fluffy baby shelduck wandering alone on the banks of the Severn. There appeared to be no adult ducks around so we took it home. When Dad saw it he reprimanded us severely. However, we built a cosy little shelter and attended the tiny bird lovingly. Sadly, after a short time, it died. We had learned a lesson but at the cost of this delightful duckling's life.

House martins

Constructing their nests of mud, house martins are master builders. They nest in colonies, preferring to nest on newer buildings with large overhangs on the eaves which provide shelter.

There was once a very large colony nesting under the stone arches of an old railway bridge over the river Severn. There was plenty of mud for nest construction and large numbers of flying insects for food. Why the birds abandoned the site remains a mystery.

House martins feed on insects caught on the wing. They hunt at a greater height than swallows but at a lower level than swifts.

Badger watching

My wife and I, with our two young daughters, used to watch badgers in nearby woods. A badger's eyesight doesn't seem to be attuned to spot intruders easily but its sense of smell is extremely acute.

Great care was necessary to approach the badger's sett up-wind. First we would look for a pigeon's feather; they were always easy to find. By pulling off a little of the downy part and allowing it to fall it was easy to determine which way even the slightest of breezes was blowing. With care, we found it possible to creep silently to within a few yards of a particular sett, even when the badgers were out.

One of our greatest pleasures was to feel as though we were an intimate part of the woodland scene itself, though sometimes, we had to tolerate the unwanted attentions of midges. Sitting quietly together, unobserved, amidst the scent of bluebells, we listened to the crowing of cock pheasants, the constant bickering of blackbirds as they tried to settle down for the night and the territorial hooting of tawny owls as they prepared to begin hunting. We heard the mysterious rustlings in the undergrowth and other unidentified sounds of the approaching night. Sometimes we glimpsed a woodmouse going about its business.

When the failing sunlight no longer touched the treetops it gradually grew darker. Sounds seemed to magnify. Then, quite often, there would be a strange and deep silence. Soon a badger would be seen cautiously emerging from the sett. It would be an adult who, after a moment or two, would lie on its back and scratch itself vigorously.

Two or three cubs would then appear to delight us with their antics. Free of the confines of the sett they would play, tumbling and scampering about and squealing joyfully, totally untroubled by any dangers there might be. While still keeping an eye on the cubs an adult, meanwhile, is concerned with domestic chores. The one illustrated is dragging a fresh pile of clean leaves into the sett to renew the bedding.

Peregrine falcon

Though some have made their eyries on lofty tower blocks and churches in cities, the peregrine is essentially a bird of wilder areas, mountains, coastal cliffs and, in winter, river estuaries.

Historically, peregrines have suffered much deliberate persecution. In the 1940's the War Department pursued a policy of killing coastal peregrines in the belief that they might kill carrier pigeons bearing important messages from war-torn Europe. Again, pigeon fanciers would not tolerate peregrines in their area as they preyed on homing pigeons. Its numbers were also drastically reduced during the 1960's due to the accumulation of persistent poisons through eating prey species contaminated with agricultural pesticides.

Much has been written about this iconic falcon, its hunting prowess and speed when it dives, but my lasting memories have been of long periods patiently waiting for hunger to induce a peregrine to move from its lofty perch.

On one occasion when watching a peregrine clinging to a crag and waiting for it to demonstrate its famous 180 mph stoop to catch some unfortunate bird in full flight, a companion nudged me and pointed across the river. There, in an open area among coppiced hazel, were four or five young fox cubs at play. We therefore turned our telescopes away from the reluctant falcon to witness far more active and interesting entertainment.

Some plant oddities

All plants of course are remarkable works of nature. Those illustrated are just a few of the many that display some peculiarity or other.

Goldilocks is a kind of buttercup with irregular flowers. Some look quite normal with five petals, others have more, some fewer or none at all, and petals may be different sizes.

The flower head of moschatel has four small blooms, each with five petals, facing north, south, east and west, giving the plant the popular name of 'town hall clock'. In addition, a single flower with four petals sits on top facing upwards.

Flowers of the butcher's broom are produced on leaf-like stems; large red berries are borne later. According to tradition, bunches of the plant were used by butchers to clean their blocks.

Among the local names of wild arum are:- cuckoo pint, lords and ladies, priest's pintle, parson-in-the-pulpit, friar's cowl, devils and angels, Adam and Eve, ramp, sweethearts, silly lovers, cows and bulls, bobbins and wake robin. Starchroot refers to the fact that its roots were once used as a source of starch. The finger-like spadix generates scent and heat to attract midges which pollinate the tiny flowers at its base.

Dodder is another curious plant. As a seedling, it is rooted in the soil, but soon assumes a parasitic life style, getting all its nutrients through suckers which attach to the stems of the host plant. It smothers its principal hosts of gorse and heather with a tangle of pink thread-like stems.

Medieval herbalists regarded the dark red flower head of great burnet as suggestive of blood. It was therefore used to staunch blood from wounds - acquiring the botanical name of Sanguisorba, meaning 'blood absorbing'.

Toothwort is another parasitic plant. Having no chlorophyll, it extracts nourishment from the roots of hazel. The scales below each pale pink flower are modified leaves and were thought to resemble teeth.

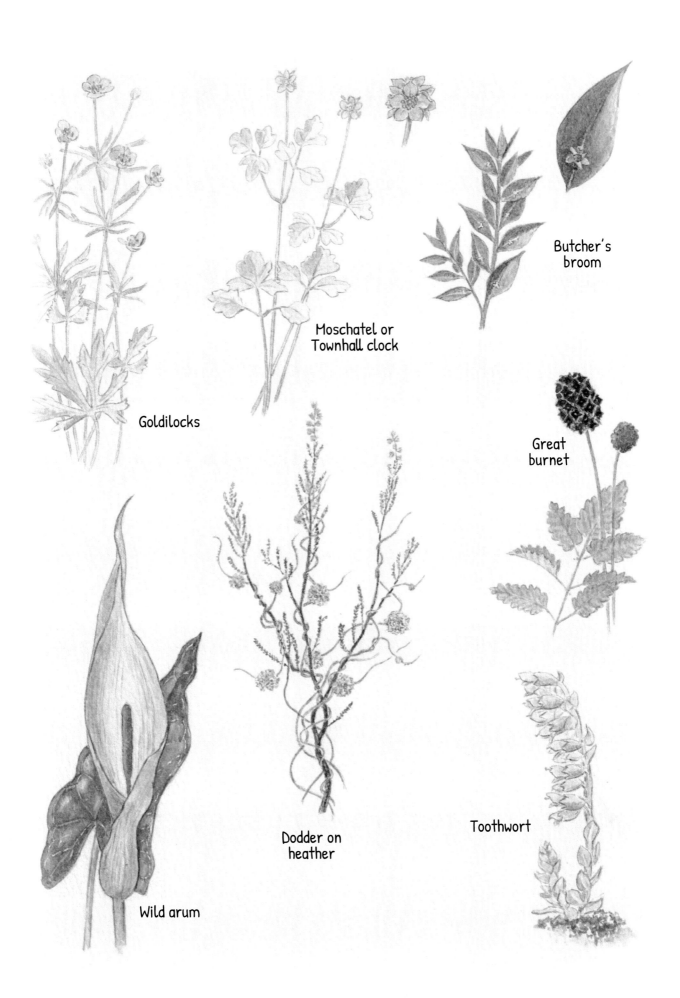

Goldilocks

Moschatel or
Townhall clock

Butcher's
broom

Great
burnet

Wild arum

Dodder on
heather

Toothwort

Bluebells

Like wild garlic and wood anemones, bluebells are plants of ancient deciduous woodland and seem to prefer damper western woods. A bluebell wood is a magnificent sight in springtime and the scent is heavenly. The flowers appear as a carpet of blue but a closer look will reveal shades of mauve and violet. You may see bees stealing nectar by biting holes into the base of the bells.

Elizabethans crushed bluebell bulbs to provide starch to stiffen the ruffs on the collars of the wealthy. Cut a bulb in half and the gummy fluid makes effective quick-drying glue. Put a couple of blooms into a wood ants nest, watch them attack with formic acid turning the flowers pink.

Vigorous Spanish bluebells hybridise readily with our native species. A survey found Spanish or hybrid plants in one in six of Britain's bluebell woods. The Spanish variety is paler, has little or no scent, and botanists are now concerned for the integrity of our native flowers.

Two woodpeckers

With specialised toes, tail feathers, beak and tongue, woodpeckers are beautifully fitted for life in their woodland habitat and their method of feeding in particular.

The colourful green woodpecker was also known as the yaffle due to its loud laughing call.

The green woodpecker, like the commoner great spotted woodpecker, probes the bark of old trees for

the larvae of wood-boring insects and other invertebrates. While the green woodpecker often feeds on ants, and their larvae, which it finds in grassland, the great spotted woodpecker will take the occasional nestling. Though the green woodpecker does drum on resonant branches, it is not nearly so much as the great spotted woodpecker which I once saw drumming on a metal pylon.

Both birds illustrated are males.

Bank vole

Spotted in a garden, this bank vole, probably a juvenile, was quietly investigating some fallen rose petals; maybe it was attracted by the scent.

I was able to crouch within a few feet of the vole which seemed mesmerised by one particular petal and appeared totally unaware of me.

It is difficult to believe that a small animal behaving so carelessly would live long; it would soon become prey to an owl, kestrel, weasel or cat.

Polypody

Rusty back

Maidenhair spleenwort

Ferns found in old walls

Wall rue

Hart's tongue

The life cycle of ferns involves two separate generations. The mature fern sheds spores from the undersides of its fronds (leaves). Germinating on a suitable moist surface, a spore may develop into a tiny heart-shaped plant called a prothalus. This structure produces male and female sex cells. Male cells swim to the female cells and after fertilisation a new fern plant grows.

I believe ferns add to the attraction and interest of old walls.

Our most familiar fern is bracken, a woodland species.

Birds' nests

There is a great variety in the nesting habits of birds.

Where food is plentiful or localised, some birds, herons, rooks, martins and notably sea birds, nest colonially, most however do not.

Some large hawks and falcons occupy nests high on a cliff ledge or tree; others nest on the ground in moorland.

Owls, tits, nuthatches, redstarts and jackdaws nest in natural holes in trees; woodpeckers may construct their own nest cavities.

Some species, such as plovers, lay eggs in scrapes on the ground in an open area with no nesting material, relying on the nest site to afford adequate protection. Such birds have the ability to feign injury in order to lure potential predators away from the area. Other birds might nest in thick tussocks of grass or a hole in the ground. The guillemot simply deposits its egg on a cliff ledge.

Wrens, chiffchaffs, woodwarblers and magpies are examples of birds that build domed nests - the most beautiful is probably that of the long-tailed tit which uses lichen and spider webs.

House martins, starlings and house sparrows etc. take advantage of man-made sites while tits, robins and owls are examples of birds that make use of nest boxes.

Most common birds however, build cup-shaped nests. Illustrated is a song thrush on its nest of dry grass and fine twigs. The thrush lines its nest with mud which becomes quite hard.

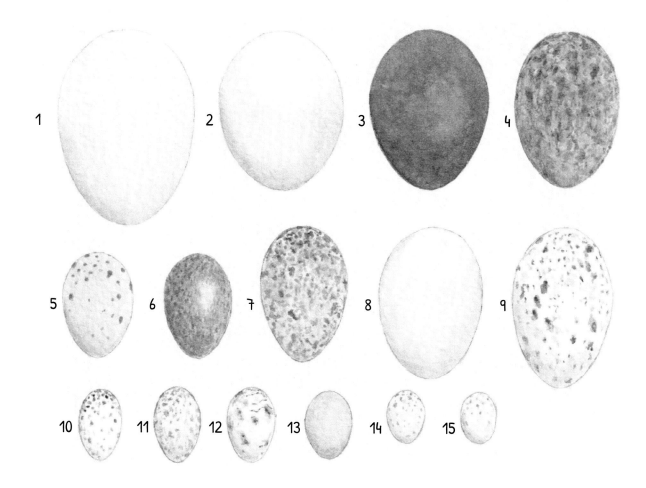

1. mallard
2. tawny owl
3. pheasant
4. crow
5. song thrush
6. blackbird
7. magpie
8. wood pigeon
9. moorhen
10. swallow
11. robin
12. chaffinch
13. dunnock
14. bluetit
15. wren

Birds' eggs

Birds generally lay their eggs well protected in nests concealed in relatively inaccessible places. While ground nesting birds tend to lay cryptically coloured eggs, some birds lay white eggs which would appear to be more open to predation. The mallard, which may lay as many as ten white eggs, covers them with down when she leaves her nest. Wood pigeons produce only two eggs, incubation beginning immediately by both sexes, so the eggs are rarely exposed. The hole-nesting tawny owl's eggs are well out of sight and will be protected by birds which can be very aggressive near their nest site.

Small birds incubate their eggs for about two weeks, when blind, naked, helpless young hatch. They need to be fed and tended for perhaps two more weeks before they fledge. In contrast, the young of pheasants, ducks and moorhens are much more highly developed when they break out of their shells and leave the nest soon after they have dried. The incubation period of these birds must therefore be longer, - about four weeks for a mallard.

Eggs can withstand strong outside pressures due to the shape and crystalline structure of the shells. However, the relatively modest force exerted by a weak chick inside is sufficient for it to break out of its shell comparatively easily.

Mallard ducklings

The mallard is the commonest duck of our inland waters. I couldn't resist stopping to watch these ducklings as they paddled around quickly on a local pond. Some were picking up morsels, which I took to be flies, off the green algae. Others, unaware of possible dangers, strayed away to explore.

Young ducklings are subject to many perils and a brood of eight or ten, which leave a nest, may soon become severely depleted in number. This was the case with this family for I counted only five a week later.

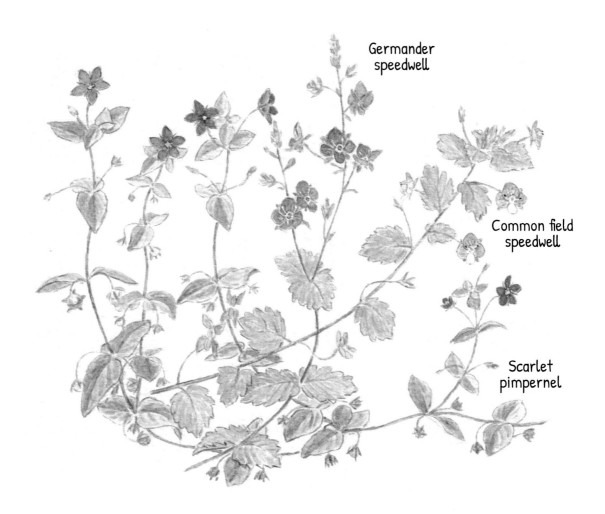

Germander speedwell

Common field speedwell

Scarlet pimpernel

Some small garden weeds

Flowering from March to July, the bright blue germander speedwell is found in grassland and as a lawn weed. The common field or Persian speedwell was introduced from Asia and flowers throughout the year if the weather is favourable. Like the common field speedwell, the scarlet pimpernel is a weed of cultivation blooming from May to August. The flowers tend to open in the morning and close by mid afternoon, if the weather is poor it remains closed. It is known as the poor man's weatherglass.

Like so many things in our wonderful natural world, one really needs to use a hand lens to appreciate the beauty of these tiny flowers.

Though they are persistent weeds, small numbers are welcomed in my garden.

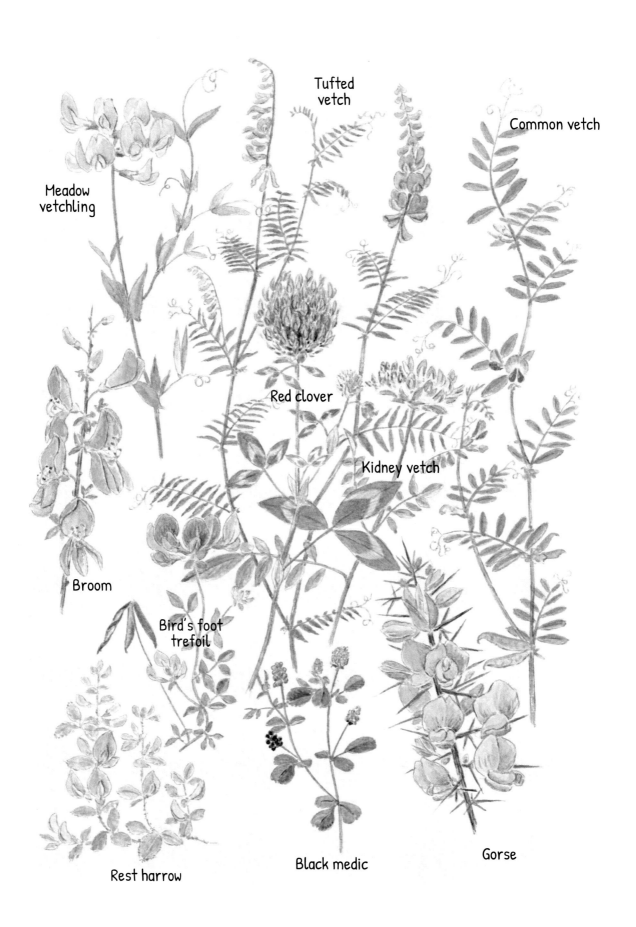

Meadow vetchling

Tufted vetch

Common vetch

Red clover

Kidney vetch

Broom

Bird's foot trefoil

Rest harrow

Black medic

Gorse

Ten flowers of the pea family

The pea family, or legumes, is one of the largest families of flowering plants and it is one of great economic importance. They are an important food source for humans and livestock. Legumes are highly valued for the high protein content of their seeds or pulses. Lucerne, vetch and clovers are important forage plants for farm animals.

Flowers of the pea family have five petals. The upper petal is normally broad and is called the 'standard'. Two smaller lateral petals are known as 'wings'. The 'keel' is made up of two lower petals, sometimes grown together forming a boat-shaped structure, or tube, enclosing the reproductive organs. The weight of an insect landing on the flower opens the keel exposing the stamens and pistil which are then able to touch the underside of the insect's abdomen. There are however, subtle differences in the details of the actual pollination of the various legume species.

Members of the pea family host certain bacteria in root nodules which convert atmospheric nitrogen into a form which plants can use. When legumes are grown as 'green manure' and the crop ploughed in, the humus content of the soil is increased while the nitrogen-rich root nodules increases soil fertility. This reduces artificial fertiliser usage.

However, it is the attractive flowers of the pea family I delight in - not least the beautifully scented garden sweet peas.

Woodcock

The woodcock is a bird of damp woodland with large clearings. It needs access to soft ground in which to probe for worms, beetles and insect larvae with its long bill. The woodcock's plumage has remarkable cryptic colouration and its eyes are set well back and high on its head permitting it an amazingly wide angle of vision. These adaptations are critical for a bird that feeds and nests on the ground in order to reduce the attentions of predators.

The woodcock remains in deep cover during the day. It is at dusk from March onwards that, as the light fades and the woodland clearing darkens, a woodcock may be seen against the sky. The bird produces a regular hoarse croaking followed by a high-pitched 'twisick' sound as it patrols the boundaries of its territory in a flight known as roding.

One afternoon in spring, while roaming in a local woodland clearing, I disturbed a woodcock. It fluttered clumsily for a few yards, as if injured, so naturally I went to where it had landed. However, it flew up again settling further away. When I approached, up it got again and again I followed. It was then I realised what was probably happening. The bird was taking me away from its nest and I never managed to locate the spot where I first disturbed it.

Biting
stonecrop

Wallflower

Ivy-leafed
toadflax

Navelwort

Yellow corydalis

Common 'wall' flowers

Biting stonecrop. This plant is also known as wall pepper as its leaves have a peppery taste. It is generally found growing on the tops of walls, also on sand dunes. It was once apparently grown on roofs in the belief that it would ward off lightning and the attentions of witches.

Wallflower. This is a member of the cabbage family. It is an introduced species from which garden varieties have been developed.

Ivy-leaved toadflax. This plant is also known as mother-of-millions. While unfertilised, the flowers are held above the leaves. After fertilisation the seed capsule moves away from the light into a dark crevice where the seeds are deposited.

Navelwort. This is so named for the depression in the, almost circular, leaf where it unites with the stem. It is commonly known as pennywort and its leaves taste like cucumber.

Yellow corydalis. Like the ivy-leaved toadflax, this was once a garden plant which 'escaped'.

Plants that thrive on walls, where it is likely to be dry, need to have adaptations enabling them to cope. Stonecrop and navelwort have thick fleshy water-retaining leaves. Wallflowers, (like other members of the cabbage family), also ivy-leaved toadflax and yellow corydalis like lime which is found in the mortar of old walls. They also have deeply penetrating roots and benefit from good drainage.

Poppies and ox-eye daisies

Poppies grow in arable fields and on disturbed ground. They flourished on First World War battle fields where they took on a profound significance. Where local road widening was taking place, corn poppies and ox-eye daisies set the roadside ablaze with scarlet, white and gold.

The common corn poppy plant is reputed to produce up to 17,000 tiny seeds in one season. These are thrown out of holes near the top of the seed heads as the long stem sways in the breeze. Seeds can remain dormant in the soil for many years and, when brought to the surface, a small percentage will germinate.

The familiar ox-eye daisy, also known as moon daisy, dog daisy or marguerite, is common in hay meadows, on waste ground and roadsides. A member of the largest family of flowering plants, the Compositae, each flower consists of an outer ring of white ray-florets, disc-florets making up the gold-coloured centre of the bloom. The seeds can remain viable in the ground for several years, the plant also spreading from rhizomes.

Poppies and daisies complement each other beautifully, though the perfect backdrop for poppies is a field of corn. It is regrettable that modern agricultural practices have put an end to the glorious sight of poppies that graced our summer cornfields for thousands of years.

Ceres, the Roman goddess of crops, has been depicted with a wreath of poppies, and poppy seeds have been found among grains of barley in 2500 year old Egyptian remains.

Bird's foot trefoil

This plant is a member of the pea family. It is quite common, flowering from June to September on short grassland. The illustration, viewed from above, is a copy of a patch on my lawn. I hope it will spread for it is one of my favourite flowers.

This enchanting little flower has many other names suggested by its shape and colour and form of its seed pods - rosey morn, lady's shoes and stockings, Tom Thumb, God almighty's thumb and finger, love entangled, crows-toes, Devil's claws, and my favourite, eggs and bacon.

Foxgloves

These stately flowers flourish on local acid soils and in a remarkably short time, after forestry operations clear-fell an area of woodland, foxgloves set it aglow with colour.

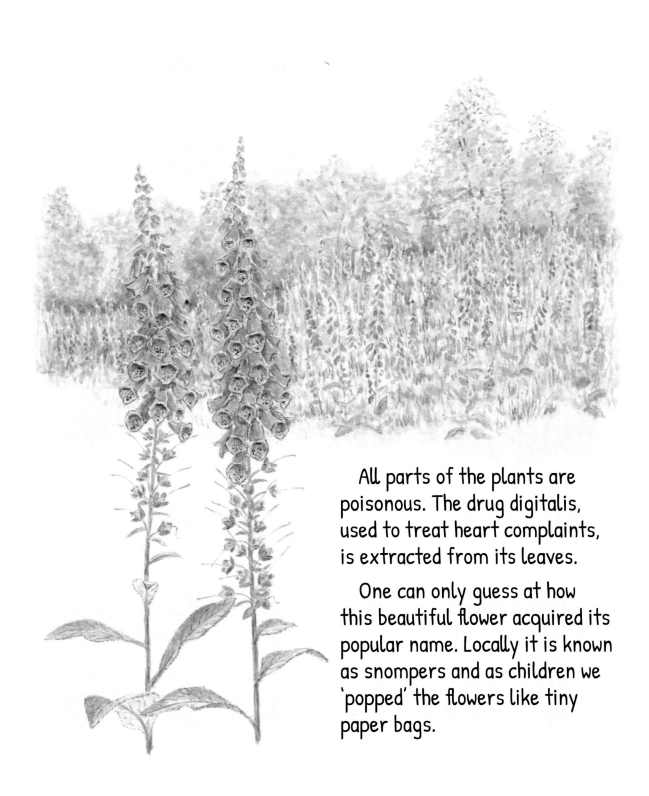

All parts of the plants are poisonous. The drug digitalis, used to treat heart complaints, is extracted from its leaves.

One can only guess at how this beautiful flower acquired its popular name. Locally it is known as snompers and as children we 'popped' the flowers like tiny paper bags.

Some little yellow flowers

Flower colour is just one common feature of these plants; all are low growing, creeping or trailing and can be found in damp grassy places. Silverweed and cinquefoil can also tolerate dry roadsides. All except yellow pimpernel are members of the rose family with the generic name of Potentilla meaning 'potent'. They were once used to treat a range of ills from ulcers to fevers and sore throats to nosebleed.

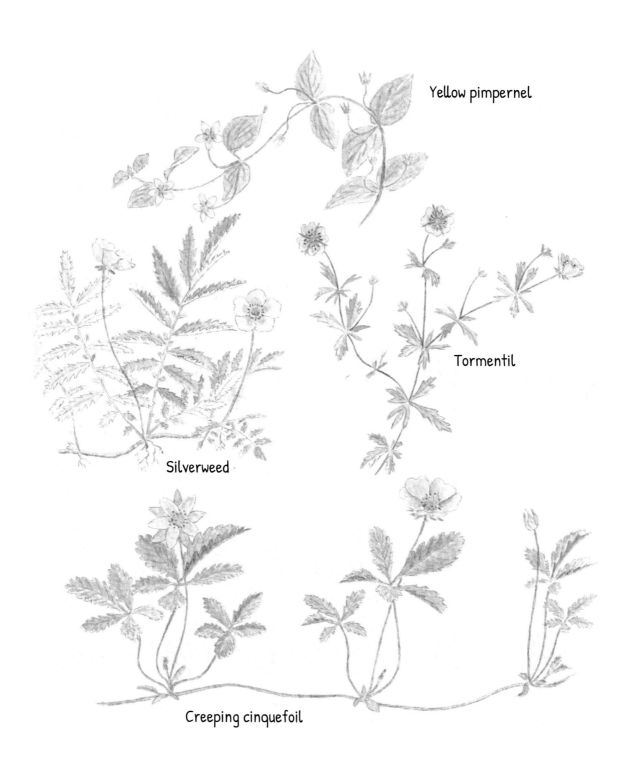

Yellow pimpernel

Tormentil

Silverweed

Creeping cinquefoil

Rabbits

Rabbits are thought to have been introduced by the Normans. Kept in purpose-built warrens they provided meat and fur. Inevitably many escaped.

Rabbits feed mainly at night. Later, in the safety of their burrows, they extract more nutrition by eating the soft droppings that have already passed through the digestive tract. The second droppings are hard and deposited above ground on latrines which are often the flattened tops of old ant hills.

Rabbits need to be vigilant for they have many enemies including foxes, badgers, stoats, buzzards, large gulls, dogs, cats and man. Large eyes on the side of the head, large directional ears and a keen sense of smell help in locating danger. If a threat is perceived, the rabbit thumps the ground with its hind feet and, as it runs for cover, the white underside of its scut (tail) serves as a signal to others. Rabbits are prolific breeders but few reach adulthood.

Nightjars

Nightjars arrive from Africa in May and settle on heathland and forest clearings with a scattering of trees. The nightjar lies motionless on the ground during daylight hours concealed by its remarkable cryptic plumage. At dusk it takes silently to the air hawking for flying insects particularly moths. It has a tiny beak but a huge gape surrounded by stiff bristles.

As the sun goes down this enigmatic bird, perched lengthwise along a branch rather than across it as other birds do, delivers its extraordinary churring song, a continuous penetrating repetition of two notes. The prolonged sound may go on for several minutes, rising and falling in volume and pitch as it does so. The effect is quite magical, the mechanical-like churring making the whole atmosphere pulsate. No wonder the bird has been associated with the activities of witches.

As a young lad, having read R.M. Ballantyne's book, The Dog Crusoe, I set out one evening to try an experiment. The hero of Ballantyne's book had hidden in bushes and waved a flag to attract the curiosity of deer in order to shoot one for food. I had tried the ruse on sheep and it seemed to work-though I didn't shoot one with my bow and arrow! Sitting on a tree stump I waved my 'rag on a stick' and very soon two nightjars began circling me just a few yards away making crackling sounds with their wings. It occurred to me that, as nightjars feed largely on night-flying moths, whose wings are often light in colour, the birds may have thought they had seen a tempting meal in the form of an unusually large moth.

As darkness came on, something to one side caught my eye. The back of my neck began to prickle, resulting in me running home, for my actions had the unintentional effect of attracting a fox that was circling me. In the gloaming it looked very much bigger to me than it should have done.

Brown hare

I saw this hare loping slowly across a piece of neglected pasture in Scotland.

Like rabbits, brown hares, having eyes set high on the sides of the head and large mobile ears, are well equipped to gain accurate information about their surroundings. Hares are larger than rabbits and almost twice as heavy. They are solitary and rest in a shallow depression, known as a form, in rank grass or plough furrow during the day. Rabbits are gregarious and dig burrows or hide in dense gorse or bramble thickets.

Rabbits give birth to litters of three to eight blind, deaf and almost naked young (kittens). Hares produce fewer, but more highly developed young, consequently the gestation period is much longer than that of rabbits.

An adult hare is able to out-run its potential enemies so the decline in numbers is probably due to the widespread use of agricultural herbicides while young hares, or leverets, may be killed by farm machinery or taken by foxes or buzzards.

Gladdon

Unlike the bright yellow flag iris, gladdon is happy in drier locations. It flowers from May to about July.

I am baffled by some authorities who describe the appearance of the blooms as 'dull' or at best, merely 'distinctive'. I grew the plant from seed found in Kent and consider the flowers very beautiful, albeit in a modest way.

The ripe fruit splits into three parts revealing bright red seeds.

When its leaves are crushed a peculiar odour is emitted. This smell is described by some as a 'stink' and by others as like that of 'roast beef'. This has earned this attractive plant two alternative unflattering names- stinking iris and roast beef plant.

Honeysuckle

Honeysuckle, also known as woodbine, is a popular climber due to its attractive flowers and their sweet scent. It is one of the earliest woody plants to come into leaf. It climbs in a clockwise direction and may reach a height of about 6 metres, often deforming plants to which it clings. The leaves are eaten by the caterpillars of the white admiral butterfly.

The exotic-looking flowers bloom from June to September. They are visited by bees during the daytime for the copious amounts of nectar they secrete. According to one authority the proboscis, or tongue, of the honey bee is between 5 and 8 mm long and that of the bumble bee 12 mm long. This means that bees can only reach part of the available nectar. Butterflies have long proboscises of about 18 mm so could probably reach the nectar but honeysuckle flowers do not provide a suitable landing platform for them.

As evening approaches, scent produced by the flowers becomes much stronger, attracting night-flying moths which feed while hovering and have long proboscises - approximately 26 mm long in the case of the humming bird hawk moth. Honeysuckle is therefore considered to be a 'moth flower' and the pale colour of the blooms make them easier to see in the poor light.

When insects visit flowers they brush past both stigma and stamens, collecting and depositing pollen as they do so, but as these organs do not ripen at the same time, cross-pollination is assured. After pollination the flowers become yellower and eventually redden. In time unpalatable red berries develop.

The nectar is absolutely delicious, no wonder the flowers were once associated with romantic love!

Three easily identified buttercups

End lobe of leaf stalked. Sepals reflexed. - bulbous buttercup.

Leaves roughly triangular, end lobe stalked, sepals erect, sends out runners. - creeping buttercup

End lobe of leaves unstalked, sepals of flowers erect. The plant is tall.- meadow buttercup

Hunting sparrowhawk

Surprise is the strategy employed by the sparrowhawk. To see the bird flying swiftly alongside a hedge, then suddenly dart up and over to the other side to burst in on a flock of terrified small birds, can be quite spectacular.

The sparrowhawk has a long tail and relatively short rounded wings enabling it to manoeuvre well in confined spaces. Occasionally one dashes through our garden causing great alarm among the resident birds. When it rests a few moments on the fence, we can see its long legs and toes. But it is its piercing, sinister, yellow eyes that grabs the attention.

The bird illustrated is a male. It takes birds the size of a finch which is a factor in keeping the numbers of small birds reasonably stable. The larger female can take birds up to pigeon size.

Dog roses

The rose family is very large, it includes brambles, strawberries, cinquefoils, hawthorn, apples and cherries etc.

With its long arching stems, the dog rose is a plant of woodland edges and is commonly found in hedgerows where its hooked thorns secure support from other plants. The plant is very variable. Flowering in May and June, most plants produce pink flowers though some may have white flowers. Its beautiful delicately scented blooms, the largest of our wild roses, is an important source of nectar, attracting many insect species. Hips mature in September and October and are eaten by birds of the thrush family.

Experts recognise over a dozen kinds of wild rose in Britain. The field rose is a common one found in similar places to the dog rose. The flowers are always white, but look different in form due to the styles being joined into a central column- a feature which often shows up as a projection on its hips.

The leaf buds of the dog rose may be infected by a tiny gall wasp causing a ragged ball of fibrous growth known as a robin's pincushion.

Modern roses are grafted on to the hardy rootstock of the dog rose (*Rosa canina*).

The pipistrelle bat

To most people bats are mysterious fascinating creatures. As a boy, I remember dozens of them hunting at dusk around the buildings of a local farm and near a church. I have also seen them hanging like plums in a cave system. Sadly, it is now unusual to see bats in our area. One recent encounter though, was rather odd and unbat-like.

On a warm sunny afternoon in midsummer I watched a small bat patrolling a woodland ride. It repeatedly fluttered up and down the track, over a length of about 40 metres, at a height of a little over 2 metres. It didn't deviate from its regular flight path to catch an insect that I could detect. As it was tiny I assumed it to be a pipistrelle which had been disturbed from its roost.

Pipistrelles hibernate from November to March in crevices in buildings and rocks or in hollow trees. They are the commonest and most widespread of our bats and are only about 3.5 cms long with a wingspan of about 20 cms.

The sophisticated echo-location system which bats are equipped with enables pipistrelles to locate and catch midges and small moths. Larger insects are enveloped in the tail membrane and all are eaten while still in flight.

Fallow deer fawn

Driving home very late one night, my wife and I saw this delightful little fawn in the middle of the road. It seemed to be utterly lost and totally bewildered. The poor little creature was very unsteady on its feet and hadn't worked out how to use its long legs effectively.

We watched it tottering uneasily on the hard surface of the road for as long as we could, until, eventually, it disappeared into the tall ferns, hopefully to join its mother.

Plants used in ancient treatments

Plants throughout history have been used in many ways, principally as food. Plants were also used as building materials, and in the cloth industry, also as a source of drugs, and masking unpleasant smells. Some had historic or religious significance, others used in love potions. Some were believed to have healing properties.

Those illustrated here were not only used as their names suggest, but in some cases were claimed to have other healing properties. Leaves of woundwort were applied to wounds to stem blood flow, its leaves were also made into ointments and poultices. Selfheal was boiled in water, sweetened and used as a gargle. Apart from treating diseases of the heart, heartsease was used to treat skin problems and as a love charm. Comfrey, or knitbone, was traditionally valued as a cure for various stomach and chest complaints, but mainly to set broken bones. The roots were grated and mixed with water to form a paste. This was placed around the broken limb where it would set hard like plaster of Paris. In the old days of sailing ships sailors had no access to fresh fruit and vegetables for long periods of time, consequently they suffered the terrible effects of scurvy. It was found that scurvy grass, rich in vitamin C, prevented the disease.

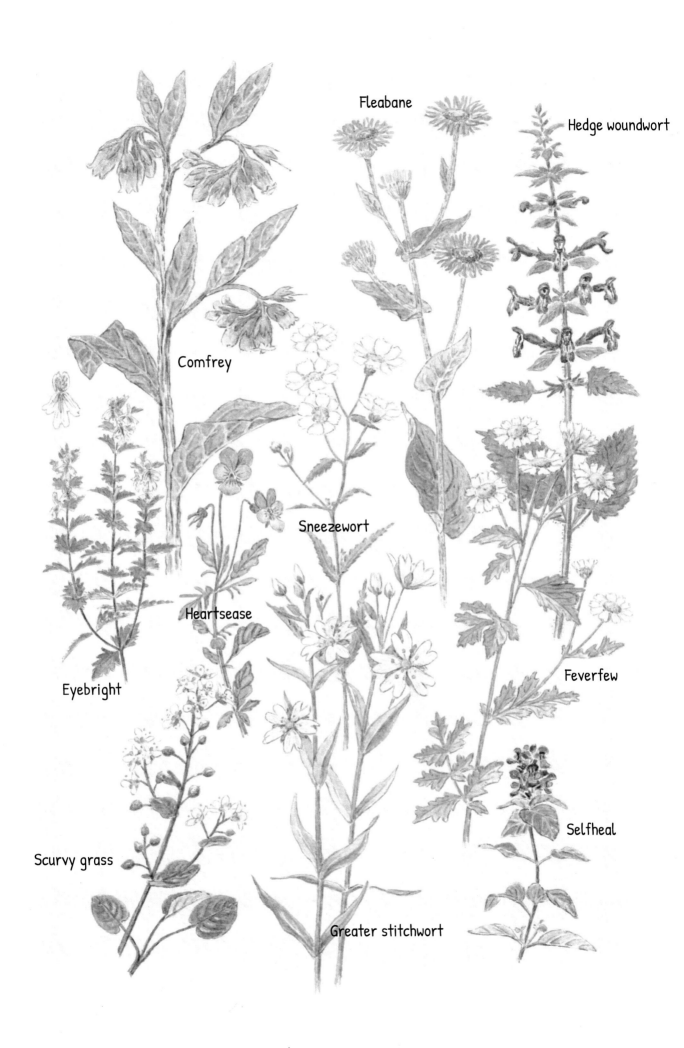

Fleabane

Hedge woundwort

Comfrey

Sneezewort

Eyebright

Heartsease

Feverfew

Scurvy grass

Selfheal

Greater stitchwort

127

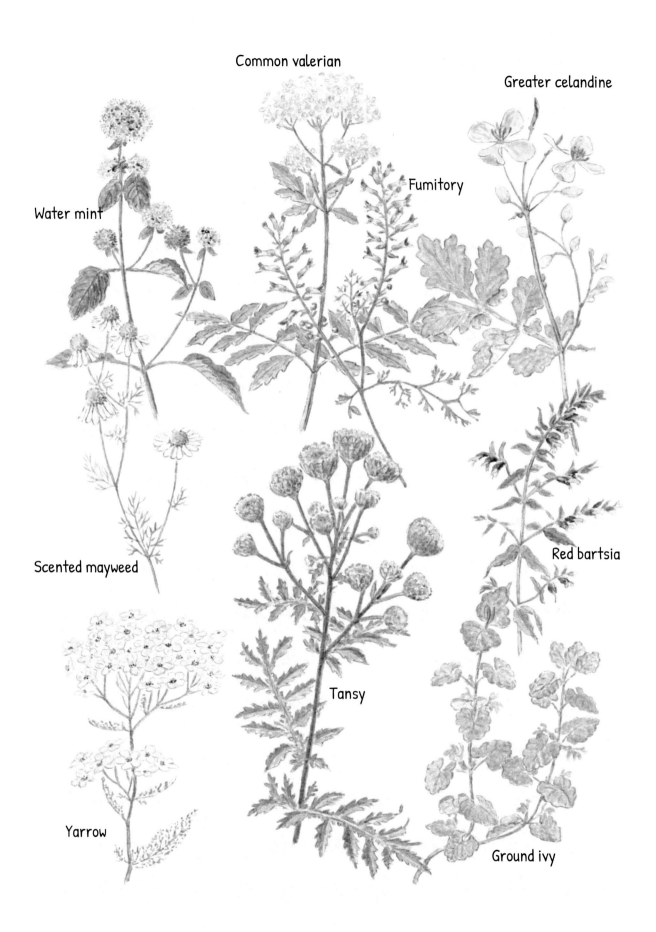

Common valerian

Greater celandine

Fumitory

Water mint

Red bartsia

Scented mayweed

Tansy

Yarrow

Ground ivy

128

More plants used in old remedies

In most cases the common names of plants do not indicate the medical cures once attributed to them. Illustrated are a few native plants that together, may once have been considered effective in treating almost any ailment.

Water mint was thought to be a cure for stomach troubles - and earache. Juice from the roots of common valerian soothed nerves, relieved headaches and aided sleep. The potent orange sap of greater celandine was effective in burning away warts and corns. Concoctions of fumitory were used to treat arthritis, gallstones, scabies, eczema and as a diuretic and laxative. Scented mayweed was thought to be good for indigestion and insomnia, while red bartsia was thought to ease toothache.

Yarrow was used for colds and to stem bleeding. It was also thought to improve one's physical appearance. Ground ivy was used for coughs, chest complaints, headaches and bruises. Many cures were attributed to tansy, including fevers, rheumatism, gout and intestinal worms. Its generic name is Tanacetum, derived from the Greek word meaning immortal, (but it could only have been the most gullible who believed drinking an infusion of tansy conferred immortality).

One should not be too cynical about the effectiveness of medieval medical treatments using native wild plants for, even now in the western world, about 40% of our prescription drugs are derived from plants that people have used for centuries.

Some authorities estimate that only 6% to 15% of the approximately 250,000 higher plant species have ever been investigated for bioactive compounds.

Musk mallow

There are several kinds of mallow growing in Britain - all with pink flowers. They are related to the stately hollyhock, the beautiful hibiscus and the useful cotton plant.

The musk mallow is so named for its musky smell. As illustrated, the upper leaves are deeply divided. However, the lower leaves are kidney-shaped and borne on long stalks.

Mallows were widely used in the past to relieve a range of health conditions.

Seashells

Rock pools are always a source of mystery and fascination and to share the experience of exploring them with a wide-eyed child is utter joy. In the water we saw many natural wonders, strange colourful seaweeds, peculiar flower-like sea anemones, tiny scuttling crabs, prawns, that were almost transparent, a small fish and, of course pretty shells. After long and delicate negotiations, my granddaughter allowed me to borrow some of the shells we had collected in order to paint them.

The shells, made of calcium carbonate, once formed hard protection for soft bodied marine molluscs. Those illustrated can be separated into two distinct types. The coiled shells belong to a class of molluscs known as gastropods (terrestrial and marine slugs and snails are also gastropods). Though cowries, common and slipper limpets, show no obvious coiling they are also gastropods. Common limpets and winkles graze green plant materials while whelks eat carrion and tower shells filter tiny food particles from the water. Hermit crabs shelter in shells which they drag around, moving into a larger one as they grow.

The remaining shells illustrated are bivalves. Normally there are two shells joined by a flexible hinge but when washed up on the shore they are often separated. The 'foot' of most bivalves is adapted for burrowing into sand or mud where they are safer from predators. The piddock however uses its tough shell to bore into soft rock or wood, filtering food particles near the entrance in safety.

Cockles, mussels, winkles and oysters have long been a food source for man. Seashells have been used in art, as ornaments, as musical instruments, even as currency in some parts of the world. Seashells are remarkable and beautiful creations, their fascination appeals not just to old men and children but is universal.

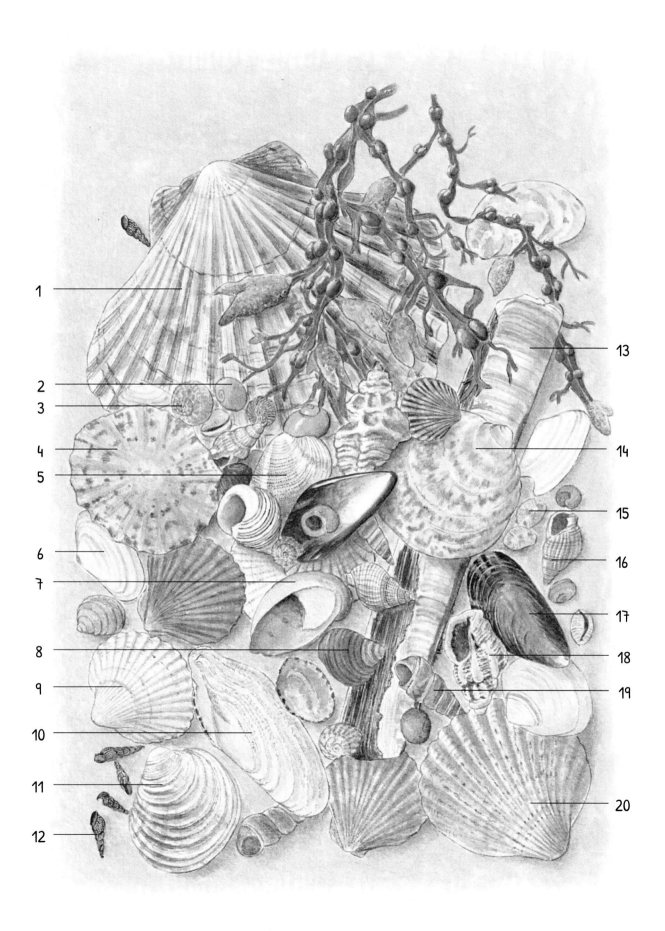

1

2
3

4
5

6
7

8

9

10

11

12

13

14

15

16

17

18

19

20

Seashells illustrated

1. great scallop
2. flat winkle
3. purple top shell
4. common limpet
5. banded carpet shell
6. banded wedge shell
7. slipper limpet
8. common winkle
9. edible cockle
10. common piddock
11. warty venus
12. needle shell
13. razor shell
14. dog cockle
15. European cowrie
16. common whelk
17. common mussel
18. sting winkle
19. tower shell
20. prickly cockle

Golden eagle

When holidaying in the Western Isles I saw a large bird soaring in the distance. It didn't seem to be quite like the buzzards I am used to seeing so I concluded that it was a golden eagle.

I created this picture in my imagination; the majestic bird perched on a lofty prominence in the 'lonely lands' of its own natural environment. It was much more appealing to me than seeing this noble bird tethered to a block in a zoo or falconry centre.

The Weasel

I had not seen a weasel for a long time when I found this one dead. Its head and body measured 19cms with a little over 4 cms more for its tail. Its close relative, the stoat, is about 5 per cent larger. I could not ascertain how the weasel had died as it had no obvious marks, so being in good condition, I took it home to draw.

A week or so later I saw one of these beautiful little carnivores dash rapidly across the lane ahead of me. Its short legs were just a blur, giving me very little chance to form an impression of it as it vanished quickly into the undergrowth.

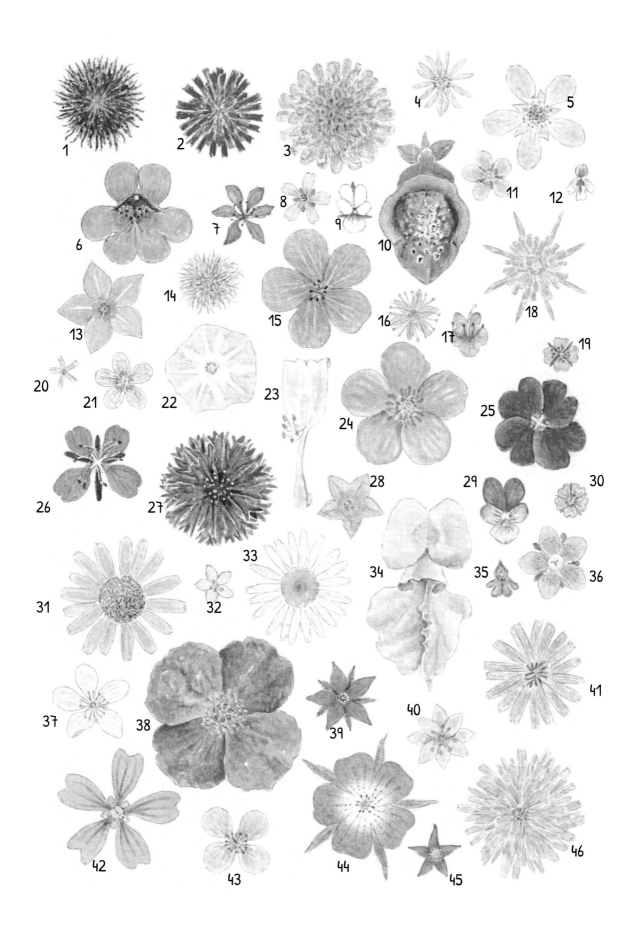

Summer flower faces

1. black knapweed
2. orange hawkweed
3. field scabious
4. sea aster
5. bramble
6. monkey flower
7. purple loosestrife
8. agrimony
9. field pansy
10. foxglove
11. silverweed
12. eyebright
13. yellow loosestrife
14. creeping thistle
15. meadow cranesbill
16. reflexed stonecrop
17. viper's bugloss
18. goatsbeard
19. tormentil
20. wall lettuce
21. white bryony
22. field bindweed
23. honeysuckle
24. greater spearwort
25. great willowherb
26. rosebay willowherb
27. cornflower
28. harebell
29. wild pansy
30. doves foot cranesbill
31. corn marigold
32. common centaury
33. scentless mayweed
34. Himalayan balsam
35. betony
36. tutsan
37. soapwort
38. long-headed poppy
39. borage
40. yellow-wort
41. chicory
42. common mallow
43. greater celandine
44. corn cockle
45. bittersweet
46. common catsear

A few local orchids

Orchids belong to probably the largest and most highly evolved family of flowering plants; there are thought to be about 24,000 species. Britain has about 50 sorts, most being found on chalk or limestone. Sadly, due to the ploughing of ancient downland and the 'improvement' of pastures, orchids are much scarcer now and some species are restricted to only a few locations in our country.

Twayblades and helleborines occur in small numbers in local woods and spotted orchids in a few meadows. Green-winged orchids can be seen in large numbers in a field which is now a county trust reserve and a few lady's tresses at the bottom of an old abandoned limestone quarry. A small colony of pyramidal orchids flourished on a local roadside verge but have now been destroyed by the council's mowing machines. A single bee orchid appeared in the wild patch in my garden some years after the delivery of a load of top soil. Now, I look forward each year to seeing a colony of about a dozen.

Orchids produce dust-like seeds, so small as to be deficient in reserves of nutrients. Germination and early growth is dependent on specific mycorrhizal fungi in the soil. Though orchid seeds are minute they are produced in vast numbers, an adaptation maximising the chance of some seeds encountering the vital mycorrhizal fungi. It has been estimated that an average heath spotted orchid produces 186,300 seeds per season while it has been claimed that one exotic species, acropera, produces up to 74,000,000 seeds.

Some orchids hybridise readily making identification problematic in some cases. There can be much variation among different colonies of pyramidal orchids for instance.

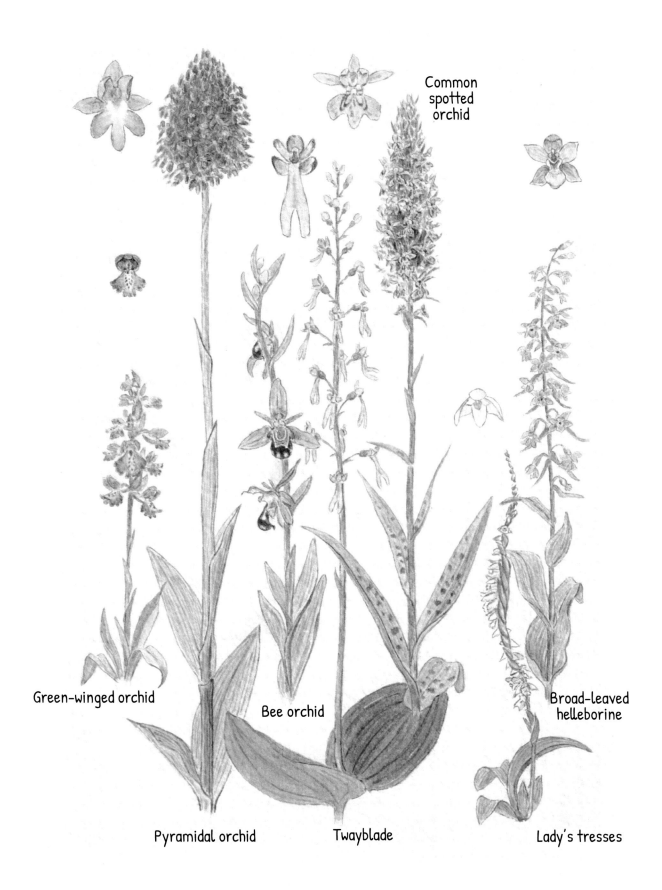

Common spotted orchid

Green-winged orchid

Bee orchid

Pyramidal orchid

Twayblade

Broad-leaved helleborine

Lady's tresses

The red-legged or French partridge

Both the native grey and red-legged partridges are principally birds of farmland. Coveys of six or eight grey, or English, partridges were fairly common in local fields when I was a boy. When disturbed, they would burst into the air and fly rapidly away together. The grey partridge has now been replaced locally by red-legs. When alarmed, red-legged partridges are very reluctant to fly but run away quickly into cover.

It has been reported that sometimes the female red-leg will lay eggs in two nests, one clutch to be incubated by her, the other by the male.

The Cormorant

With a fairly lively sea behind it, this bird obligingly posed for me. Its appearance made it easy to accept that birds evolved from reptiles.

Cormorants are found on rocky coasts, they can also be seen on lakes and rivers inland, where they nest and roost in trees. Colonies of roosting cormorants may kill the trees with their acidic faeces.

All four toes of a cormorant's foot are joined by webbing, making very effective paddles. The feet are well back on the body, enabling the bird to pursue fish rapidly under water. On resurfacing it perches with its wings hanging out to dry as it doesn't produce the oily waterproofing of other sea birds.

In China and Japan the fishing skills of cormorants are exploited by rural fishermen. The birds are tethered to a crude boat or bamboo raft and are free to catch fish but are unable to swallow them due to their necks being artificially constricted by the fishermen.

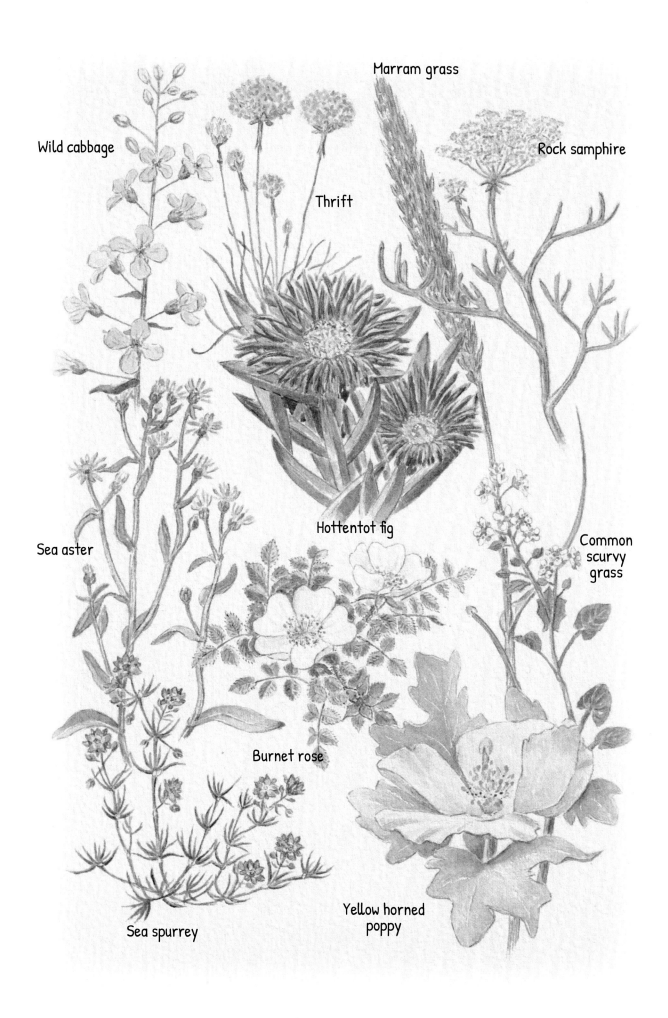

Marram grass

Wild cabbage

Rock samphire

Thrift

Sea aster

Hottentot fig

Common scurvy grass

Burnet rose

Sea spurrey

Yellow horned poppy

Ten coastal plants

Some coastal plants species may be found on cliff tops, others among rocks, on shingle, sand or mud. Salt tends to draw water out of plant cells and in order to tolerate salt spray many coastal plants have thick fleshy leaves.

Marram grass, so important for preventing coastal erosion, has fine waxy leaves which fold inwards presenting a smaller area against hot drying winds.

I found rock samphire growing out of a sea wall. One of the carrot family it was once widely eaten.

The hottentot fig, with its leaves of triangular section, is from South Africa. It clothes cliff tops in the south west and bears yellow flowers as well as cerise.

I saw scurvy grass growing with sea asters on the muddy banks of the Severn estuary. It is not a grass but is a member of the cabbage family.

Lesser sea spurrey is a lowly prostrate plant of salt marshes, muddy shores and shingle, and like scurvy grass, also grows along the sides of salted roads.

Sea asters are very attractive though some plants are without the female outer ray florets so have no petals.

The yellow horned-poppy is named from its extremely long curved pods – up to 25 cms – quite unlike the familiar seed pods of field poppies. It normally grows on shingle

The burnet rose is the spiniest of all roses. Rose hips are generally red but those of the burnet are almost black.

Thrift or sea pink can carpet cliff tops. Often grown in gardens it was depicted on pre-decimal threepenny coins.

Wild cabbages like limey soils and are common on the chalky cliffs of Dover. They are the ancestors of garden cultivars, such as cauliflowers and brussel sprouts etc.

Kingfisher

A walk along a river or canal bank in summer is always a pleasure. Besides the luxuriant display of colourful waterside plants to enjoy, one might hear the distinctive 'plop' of a water vole as it enters the water and encounter a variety of birds found only in this unique watery habitat. A flash of electric blue identifies a kingfisher as it streaks downstream uttering a high-pitched piping sound as if to warn other creatures to get out of its way. Wait a few minutes and it is likely to return.

The kingfisher is the most brilliantly coloured of our native birds. It is stoutly built with a large head and long beak and rather shy by nature. It inhabits lakes, slow-flowing rivers and streams, and in hard winters, may retreat to the coast. Its food consists of aquatic insects, tadpoles and small fish. Having dived to catch a fish, the bird stuns it by beating it on its perch then swallows it head first so that scales and fins lie flat.

The kingfisher excavates a tunnel and nest chamber in a waterside bank. The nest chamber has poor ventilation and soon becomes fouled with discarded bones.

I once found a dead kingfisher in good condition, but having failed to find a person competent enough to preserve it, I tackled the job myself. It proved to be a very unpleasant task and one I shall never repeat. I cut the side of its breast open and stuffed the bird with tissue paper - inserting black beads as eyes. Mounted on a stick it looked less than satisfactory and completely lifeless. It was displayed in a school for several years but what a sad contrast it made to the jewel-like living bird!

Redstart and Pied flycatcher

These beautiful little birds nested near our home when I was a young lad. Both species migrate from Africa favouring oak woodland in Wales and the West of England; both nest in cavities, lay light blue eggs and compete with tits for nest boxes.

My first experience of redstarts was when a pair nested in a rough stone wall that held back waste from a small coal mining operation. The nest was little more than a metre off the ground and it was easy to watch the birds as they flicked their tails rapidly up and down. These stunning birds were known locally as firebrands.

Slightly smaller than the redstart, the pied flycatcher is another eye-catching bird. We passed its nest on our way to and from school. Its numbers in our area increased in the 1940's as a result of research by the ornithologist Dr. Bruce Campbell when it was found that they took readily to nest boxes - and there was an abundance of food particularly the larvae of the green oak tortrix moth.

This little bird had great significance for me as a boy for it was the first bird I attempted to draw and I well remember watching a group of youngsters lined up on a branch just outside the nest cavity being fed in turn by their busy parents.

The whitethroat

This beautiful little warbler is one of my favourite birds. I have pictured it as I last saw it, on a tangle of wild clematis. It was known locally as the nettlecreeper or the hay bird, for it builds its nest low down in cover - a deep cup of dry grass lined with hair.

The male announces itself with a brief scratchy song from deep cover, hedge top or during a dancing display flight.

Quite common when I was a boy, numbers crashed following a drought in 1969 in Central Africa where it overwinters.

Squirrels

The grey and red squirrels are similar in several ways. Both take a wide variety of food, nuts, beech mast, buds, conifer seeds and fungi etc. They spend a great deal of time on the ground and bury surplus food for future consumption – though much may not be recovered. When disturbed, they seek refuge in tree tops where their bushy tails become essential organs of balance.

They communicate by barking, chattering and purring, flicking their tails vigorously when excited.

Grey squirrels, introduced from America, strip bark from young trees especially sycamore and beech to get at the nutritious sapwood. Common and adaptable, grey squirrels display amazing dexterity when stealing food from bird feeders.

Red squirrels are significantly smaller than greys and found in only a few areas in Britain, for example the Isle of Wight and Brownsea Island. They prefer large undisturbed forest especially of Scots pine.

Herring gulls

Behaving like a gang of
unruly ruffians and buoyed
by the updraft in the lee of a cliff
face, these bold opportunists were
patrolling a holiday seafront looking
for anything edible. It might be the remains of a
packet of fish and chips, a discarded sandwich or even
an ice-cream snatched from the hands of an unwary child,
compounding the offence with loud laughing sounds.

Their natural food consists of shellfish, crustaceans, carrion etc. and
they are attracted to municipal dumps.

Herring gulls cause concern with their increasing presence in urban
areas due to the noise and fouling they cause and the use of city roof tops
as nesting sites.

Hawfinch

Crossbill

Lesser redpoll

Chaffinch

Greenfinch

Siskin

Bullfinch

Linnet

Goldfinch

Brambling

Ten finches – the more colourful males are illustrated

The beaks of different bird species are suited to the sort of food they take. One might contrast, for instance, the long probing beak of the curlew with the broad bill of the mallard or the hooked beak of the buzzard.

Charles Darwin was interested in the beak shapes and diets of finches in the Galapagos Islands and his observations were important in forming his ideas on natural selection and evolution. Our native finches also show beak adaptations related to their particular food preferences. Finches are characterised by short sturdy bills for crushing seeds, which are supplemented by insect larvae and fruit.

The chaffinch, our commonest finch, has a generalised diet. It likes seeds and often feeds on the ground. It may be joined by migrant bramblings in winter to feed on beech mast. Linnets will also feed on the ground but prefer grain.

Siskins and redpolls are small finches with finer bills. They regularly flock together in winter acrobatically picking seeds off the slender twigs of birch and alder.

The tweezer-like bill of the goldfinch enables it to manipulate the tiny seeds of thistles, burdock and knapweed etc. In contrast, greenfinches and bullfinches tackle larger seeds with stout beaks. The bullfinch can also be destructive in orchards, taking buds of fruit trees. The large head of the hawfinch houses such powerful musculature that it can crush hard seeds like hornbeam and some authorities claim even cherry stones.

The crossbill will consume seeds of rowan and hawthorn etc, also insects, but its diet consists mainly of conifer seeds, spruce, larch and pine. Its uniquely crossed mandibles equips it to prise seeds from their cones. Such dry food necessitates the intake of water which the bird finds in woodland ponds and puddles.

Roe deer

Roe deer, the smallest of our native deer, are beautiful dainty animals. It is thought that in the Middle Ages they were widespread. Then, apparently, they 'disappeared'. Re-introductions were made about 150 years ago.

Holidaying with a forester's family in Northumberland we often saw roe deer. Adjoining the house was a large paddock that three or four deer visited with great regularity at dusk. They would browse and seemed particularly fond of the leaves and shoots of bramble. If disturbed, we saw these secretive animals leap over a low fence to disappear into the security of the forest. At other times they simply seemed to vanish, as if by magic, into the gloom.

Illustrated is a deer as I saw it in full daylight. It is a roebuck; females (does), do not have antlers.

Brown trout

A tiny group of small trout can often be seen facing the current in a particular part of a local stream. The stream is small and shallow which might be a problem for the fish as the water temperature could vary significantly. Excessively warm water might result in a reduction of oxygen levels and the possible death of the trout. Fortunately the flow of the water in the brook is quite rapid and remains cool for it emerges from an area of dense woodland where very little sunlight reaches the ground.

I often feel compelled to count the small fish but generally give up, being frustrated by rippling water, shadows, reflections and the movement of the fish themselves, which may be slow, but can also be very quick as they dart for safety.

The heron

The heron is a solitary hunter often seen poised motionless in the shallows of a river, lake, or on the sea coast, its head drawn back, as if it were a coiled spring, waiting patiently for a fish or other prey item to swim within reach. Or it can be seen carefully stalking near the bank. When it spots a likely morsel its long flexible neck shoots out like an arrow from a bow as it strikes at great speed with its dagger-like beak. If its victim is sizeable, the heron may need to manipulate the unfortunate creature before swallowing it whole. Frogs, newts, insects, crustaceans, and even small mammals and ducklings are taken. But the major part of a heron's food consists of fish which are swallowed head first. They will also take ornamental fish from urban ponds, much to the annoyance of pond owners.

The heron's long neck allows it to preen effectively but frogs, newts and fish are covered with slime which can foul the bird's feathers. The heron's breast feathers produce a fine powder which it spreads over itself. The powder soaks up slime from the feathers which is then scraped off by the serrated inner margins of the bird's long central toes.

The numbers of herons plummet in hard winters when frozen ponds and lakes lock up their main food source.

Though herons fish in a silent solitary way they nest in colonies, usually in the tops of tall trees. Such heronries can be noisy, raucous places.

Grasses

Grasses make up one of the largest groups of flowering plants. They clothe vast areas of the world. Some species thrive on heavy wet clays, others on limestone; they tolerate a wide range of temperatures and prevent soil erosion.

The grass family includes wheat, barley, oats, rye, maize, rice, millet, sorghum, sugar cane and bamboo. There are thought to be over 150 wild grass species in Britain. They have tiny complex flowers which are wind pollinated.

Grass is the most abundant crop grown in Britain and is of enormous importance in supplying the needs of man.

Cereals are a major source of carbohydrates and protein for humans, while grass is the main food of farm animals. Therefore our supply of vital products such as milk, meat, leather and wool, even beer, ultimately depend upon grass.

Wild animals too, rely on grass and the larvae of many butterfly and moth species feed on grasses, some overwintering as larvae or pupae. Indeed very many lowly invertebrate species inhabit long grass thus providing a vital link in the food chain to the benefit of higher animals and birds.

Some coarse grasses, such as bromes, are not relished by livestock; moreover couch grass, black-bent and wild oats are regarded as weeds. British farmers, therefore, tend to favour about six varieties to satisfy their needs for grazing, and cutting for hay and silage. These grasses include cocksfoot, timothy, rye grasses and fescues.

Grasses can withstand grazing by animals and mechanical cutting because new growth comes from the base of the plants.

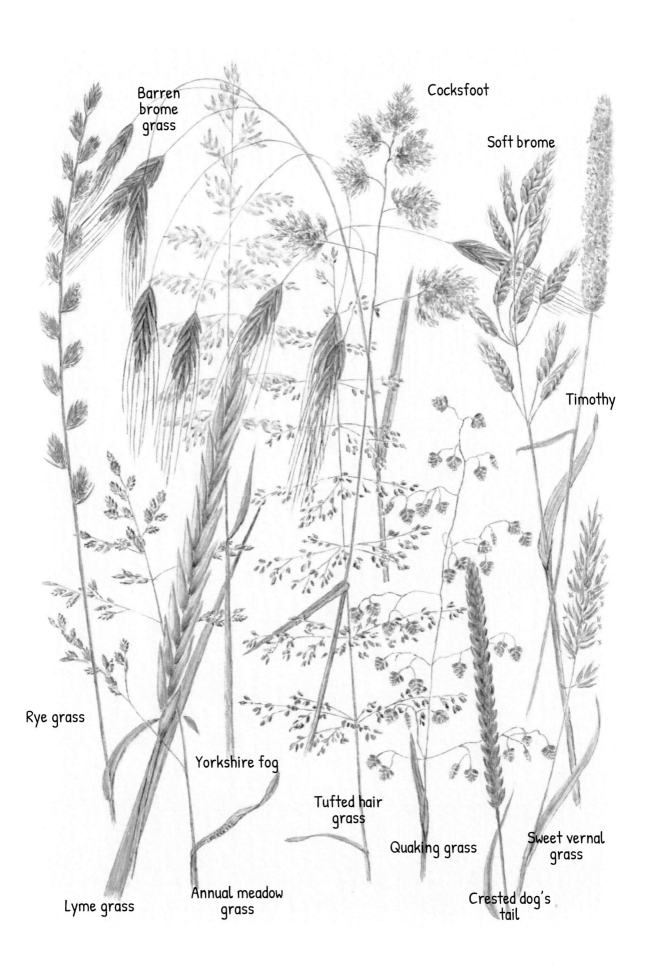

Barren brome grass

Cocksfoot

Soft brome

Timothy

Rye grass

Yorkshire fog

Tufted hair grass

Quaking grass

Sweet vernal grass

Lyme grass

Annual meadow grass

Crested dog's tail

157

Catsear, Sheepsbit and Stonecrop

This little scene caught my eye while walking in the hills of North Wales. In a valley, and sheltered by rocks, catsear, sheepsbit and English stonecrop were flourishing among clumps of moss and grasses.

Catsear is a member of the large daisy family, while sheepsbit, looking like a scabious, belongs to the campanula family. Both plants may be found in dry grassy places.

English stonecrop has round fleshy leaves so the plants can tolerate very dry conditions. Stonecrop will even grow on rocks and walls and is used on 'green' roofs.

People are attracted to scenic landscapes. These are generally wide open spaces with foreground, middle distance and far distance interest. My daughters and perhaps children generally, seemed to find pleasure in more intimate scenes. They looked joyfully on mossy banks, little falls of water and tiny colourful flowers. With the imagination stimulated, the location would soon be peopled by Lilliputian figures, perhaps fairies, and a complete story would evolve. Or the child, with Beatrix Potter-like ingenuity, might envisage a family of tiny mice living in complete harmony, in their natural surroundings, with all their requirements fully met.

My daughters taught me to delight in small scenes too.

Gatekeeper on
Bramble

♂

Brimstone on
Ivy

♂

Small skipper on
Thistle

Orange tip on
Lady's smock
♂

Ringlet on
Ribwort

♀

Holly blue on
Hawthorn

Clouded yellow
on Red clover

Marbled white
on Knapweed

♀

Silver-washed
Fritillary on
Bracken

Comma on Bramble
flowers

Red Admiral
on a plum

Butterflies

Butterflies and moths belong to the order *Lepidoptera*. Their wings are covered with tiny scales giving them their characteristic colours and patterns.

Butterflies, being more active by day and generally more brightly coloured than moths, are better known, though moth species greatly outnumber butterflies.

Moths rest with their wings folded roof-like over the body. Most butterflies hold their wings vertically above the body, the exception being skippers who position their wings at an angle. When basking in the sunshine butterflies hold their wings wide open.

Butterflies need sugary nectar to provide the energy for flight. This is obtained from flowers though some insects, especially red admirals, like rotting fruit, especially plums. Nectar is sucked up through the long flexible hollow tongue or proboscis which is neatly coiled up when not in use. When visiting flowers butterflies may also be pollinating them by transferring pollen from their hairy bodies.

Each butterfly species has a limited range of plants on which it will lay its eggs. The related species known as browns which include wall browns, speckled woods and gatekeepers lay eggs on grasses which the emerging caterpillars feed on. Violets are the food plants of fritillaries while stinging nettles are the food plants of the peacock, small tortoiseshell, red admiral and comma. It is well known that the caterpillars of large white and small white butterflies can be serious pests on cabbages and other brassicas, they also eat nasturtium leaves. The large white lays batches of about fifty eggs while the small white lays eggs singly. One wonders which is the best survival strategy.

Butterflies – winter survival

Butterflies are associated with warm summer days but how do these beautiful delicate insects survive the cold of winter ?

The life cycle of a butterfly has four stages, egg, caterpillar (larva), chrysalis (pupa) and adult (imago). Butterflies and moths have evolved various strategies to survive winter.

Most species, including all the browns, overwinter as caterpillars low down in vegetation on their particular food plants and may become active on mild days. They are ready to continue eating again when the weather becomes favourable.

The white butterflies, including the orange tip, survive at the chrysalis stage while about nine species found in Britain remain throughout the winter as eggs.

Some species, including the peacock, small tortoiseshell, red admiral and comma, spend their winter as adults in a state of torpor finding a cool, safe spot in a hollow tree or perhaps a shed. Most years on a warm day in early March I see one of those species, usually a peacock, fluttering against the window of my shed trying to get out. The brimstone shelters in dense ivy and is usually the first butterfly on the wing in springtime.

The clouded yellow and painted lady migrate to Britain from North Africa and Southern Europe in the spring, sometimes in large numbers. I remember the influx of clouded yellows in 1947, a butterfly new to me then. In 2009 there was a huge migration of painted ladies. Neither of these two beautiful butterflies is thought to be able to endure a British winter, though there is now strong evidence to suggest that, after reproducing, the progeny of the painted lady undergo the return journey.

Painted lady on Catmint

♂ Small white

Large white

♀

Small tortoiseshell on Verbena

Small heath on Agrimony

♀

Meadow brown on Meadow grass

Common blue on Trefoil

♂

Small copper on Fleabane

Peacock on Sedum

♀ Speckled wood on Bramble

Tawny owl

The tawny owl is a nocturnal hunter feeding on a variety of small mammals, the occasional bird, frogs and earthworms. It is very well equipped for its particular life style.

It can turn its head through a very wide angle bringing its amazing visual and auditory senses into a position to more accurately locate its victim.

Large sensitive, forward looking eyes, effective in low light conditions, give the bird binocular vision. Its ears are positioned asymmetrically, behind its facial discs, enabling excellent directional hearing to pinpoint the faint sounds that betray its prey.

The tawny owl has soft velvety plumage and its primary wing feathers have comb-like leading edges permitting it to fly silently.

Sharp talons and reversible outer toes ensure a firm grip on its prey. Hawks, falcons and eagles tear their food up, holding the carcass with their feet which are not feathered. By swallowing their victims whole owls avoid contaminating their feathered legs and toes.

Birds become agitated when their nests are threatened. Some species try to lure one away, others scold loudly, terns dive at intruders to drive them away. Tawny owls will attack, as my brother found when, as a boy, he climbed to investigate a tawny's nest. Very soon he was sent running home with his ears bleeding. Eric Hosking was a famous innovative pioneer of bird photography but was similarly attacked by a tawny owl. It cost him an eye. Nevertheless owls hold a special appeal for us, perhaps it is due to the cat-like forward looking eyes.

Hedgehog

Hedgehogs can sometimes be heard snuffling noisily as they forage for slugs, snails, earthworms, caterpillars and beetles. They can run quite quickly, climb pretty well and can swim, but may drown in a garden pond if there is no easy way to climb out.

Having built up body fat during the autumn, hedgehogs hibernate during the winter, though they will hunt if the weather warms up. Their ability to roll into a spiny ball at the threat of danger ensures good protection from predators but offers none from motor vehicles, which must be a factor in their decreasing numbers.

Sometimes animals do strange things which baffle scientists. It is fanciful to believe that hedgehogs pick up apples on their spines, or drink milk directly from a cow as folklore suggests. That a hedgehog has been seen to walk repeatedly around the perimeter of a circular drain cover is more plausible. No one seems to know why hedgehogs spread frothy saliva over their fur and spines but photographs do exist of this strange activity.

Harebells with bent grass

A short list of my favourite wild flowers would certainly include harebells. These gorgeous plants with their delicate nodding bell-shaped flowers of sky-blue have much to commend them. Perhaps they are at their best in a loose clump with fine grasses on a sunny bank.

Harebells are said to grow on almost any undisturbed soil, acid or chalk, yet they are sadly very scarce in our locality.

Cliff-top plants

I saw these plants growing together next to a pavement at a seaside resort in midsummer. I attempted to portray the scene faithfully but left out the protective fence for it was on a cliff top. In the background where the cliff fell almost vertically to the sea there was a dense growth of gorse, with some brambles, providing a certain amount of shelter.

The plants were a diverse mixture: wild carrot, sea aster, ragwort and common mallow, - with ribwort, hare's foot clover and a stonecrop species in the foreground. All were flourishing, while further along the cliff top thrift and sea campion were growing.

I found it odd to see sea asters, plants normally found in salt marshes, growing in close proximity to stonecrop which, having thick fleshy leaves, is adapted to tolerate dry conditions.

Some of the flower heads (umbels) of wild carrot display a central pink flower. It has been suggested that it may act as a lure to attract pollinating insects.

A relative of ribwort plantain, the greater plantain, or rat's tail, which has larger rounded leaves, was known as white man's foot by Red Indians as it was found wherever early European settlers to America had passed.

Gorse can be found in flower at any time of the year hence the old saying, 'When gorse is in flower, kissing is in season.'

Wet and dry

Smooth newt

I found these two smooth or common newts hiding under stones in the garden. They are terrestrial animals but, as amphibians, need to keep their skins moist. They breed in my garden pond but, unlike frogs and toads, lay their eggs singly, wrapped in leaves of underwater plants.

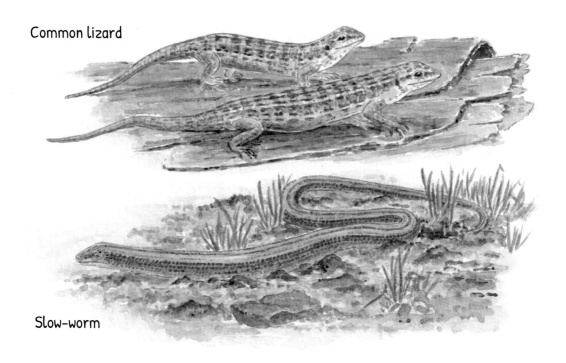

Common lizard

Slow-worm

Lizards are reptiles. They look superficially like newts but have dry scaly skins. They can sometimes be spotted basking in the sun on a log or stone. When disturbed they run swiftly into cover.

The snake-like slow-worm is a legless lizard. I saw this one crossing a woodland track. If attacked or threatened a lizard can shed its tail and, while the predator is distracted by the shed portion, make its escape.

Buzzards

These large birds of prey were rarities in West Gloucestershire when I was a boy. Certainly there would have been plenty of food for buzzards at the time, small mammals such as mice, voles, and rabbits (buzzards will also take worms, insects and carrion). Reasons for their scarcity from the mid 1950s are more easily accounted for. Myxomatosis decimated the rabbit population making it difficult for buzzards to survive. At the same time agricultural pesticides severely reduced the reproductive capacity of the birds; the chemicals were not withdrawn until the 1960s. It was not until the 1970s that buzzards began breeding in the area again and are now common.

Buzzards are highly visible birds and are often seen soaring, perched on a fence post or telegraph pole or, on some occasions, hovering.

Nuthatch

The nuthatch is a stocky little bird well adapted to life in deciduous or mixed woodland. Its clear, far-carrying, boyish whistle is quite distinctive. It is adept at climbing up or down tree trunks, head first.

Nuthatches nest in holes in trees and are unique among British birds in reducing the size of the entrance hole with mud which dries very hard.

They have a habit of wedging nuts in a crevice and splitting them open with their powerful bills to get at the kernels inside. They will also take beetles, earwigs and other small invertebrates.

Treecreeper

In contrast, the treecreeper is diminutive and unobtrusive. Its song is thin and high-pitched. Starting near the base of a tree it looks like a feathered mouse as it climbs jerkily, often in a spiral, bracing itself with its stiff tail. It always climbs up, never down like the nuthatch. It uses its fine downward pointing forceps-like bill to pick up spiders, insects and their larvae from the bark of the tree. The treecreeper roosts and nests in large cracks in tree trunks or behind loose bark.

Moths

The vast majority of Lepidoptera are moths and even though many people consider butterflies more beautiful there are a number of conventionally pretty moths. Many moths though, do look drab, but their wing patterns can be distinctive and often account for their popular names. Most of the moths illustrated were found in my small garden and represent the many hundreds of species found in Britain.

Most hawk moth species have very long proboscises (tongues), and feed while hovering at flowers. Tussock moths and swift moths have no proboscis so rely on the store of energy acquired by their larval stages.

Hawk moths, unable to survive a British winter, migrate from Southern Europe and North Africa. In contrast, the winter moth illustrated, was seen outside my kitchen window at the end of December. The female of this species has vestigal wings only, while females of some moths have no wings at all.

Moths, known as swift moths, are fast fliers, others, such as cinnabars and burnets flutter slowly. They display warning colours and produce distasteful poisons. Brightly coloured moths tend to fly by day; nocturnally active moths are generally relatively dingy in appearance. The buff tip looks like a broken twig when at rest. Geometer moth larvae known as loopers, because of the way they crawl, assume a twig-like posture when at rest. The long hairs of some moth caterpillars deter most birds and can result in a rash if handled by humans.

Some species can be serious pests. Large numbers of green oak tortrix caterpillars for example, can defoliate oak trees. They protect themselves from the attentions of small birds by curling oak leaves into shelters or hanging from silk threads.

Moths constitute an incredibly fascinating part of our natural world.

Thirty moths identified

1. buff ermine
2. six-spot burnet
3. dot moth
4. small magpie
5. winter moth
6. common marbled carpet
7. cinnabar moth
8. common footman
9. shuttle-shaped dart
10. yellow shell
11. angle shades
12. red underwing
13. silver Y
14. Nemophora degeerella
15. green oak tortrix
16. hummingbird hawkmoth
17. cabbage moth
18. heart and dart
19. scarlet tiger
20. pale tussock moth
21. carpet moth
22. Jersey tiger
23. white plume moth
24. ruby tiger
25. white-line dart
26. feathered gothic
27. chimney sweeper
28. buff tip
29. plain wave
30. ghost swift

Black and white

Several different families of birds are represented in these illustrations. All are associated with the seashore in some way, whether it is rocky coastline, sheltered inlets or muddy or sandy bays. But why are the colours black and white so common among water birds? Birds of inland waters could be included also, for example the moorhen, dipper and tufted duck. There are exceptions of course, notably most waders and many ducks.

It has been suggested that the white undersides of many water birds makes it more difficult, when they are swimming, for potential aquatic predators to see them from below. Again there are exceptions, such as the dark plumage of the cormorant.

It seems unlikely that the colour of plumage has a major part to play in seabird courtship except in ducks, though the colours of beaks and feet may be significant. Rather it is the physical courtship displays that initiate and maintain pair bonding.

It is thought that the black pigment melanin in feathers make them more durable and resistant to wear. Some gulls, for instance, have primary wing feathers tipped with black, though many do not. Guillemots and other birds of the auk family spend a great deal of time on rocky cliffs where their wings and tails are at risk of severe abrasion, perhaps this is one of the reasons for their feathers being black.

Common tern

Puffin

Guillemot

Great black-backed gull

Gannet

Cormorant

Avocet

Oystercatcher

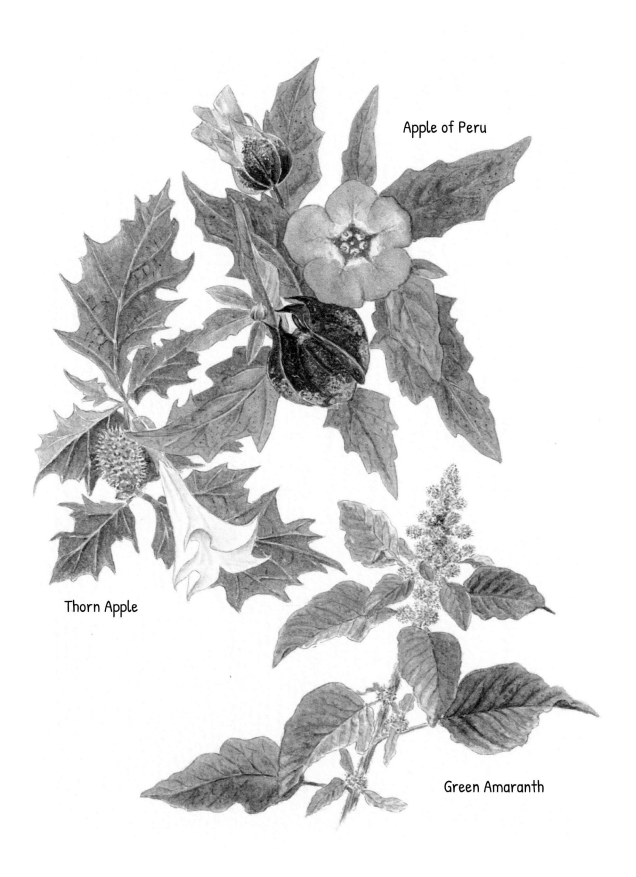

Apple of Peru

Thorn Apple

Green Amaranth

178

Three aliens

When a strange plant appears in my garden I let it grow undisturbed. One such stranger was the apple of Peru. It is a member of the solanaceae which includes potatoes, tomatoes and night shades. The leaves have many tiny black spots from which short stiff hairs protrude. This, together with largely black fruits give the plant a rather sinister look, though the flowers are pretty. All parts of the plant are said to be poisonous. Indeed it is an insect repellent, having the alternative name of shoo-fly. The plant was originally introduced to Britain as a garden flower.

Following a long hot summer another exotic-looking invader appeared in my garden. The thornapple, another solonaceae, and almost identical in appearance to the apple of Peru but its trumpet-shaped flowers and its spiny fruit are unique identifying features. Again, all parts, particularly the seeds, are poisonous and have hallucinogenic properties. The thornapple is widely naturalised in warmer countries throughout the world.

A much more benign alien which has appeared in my garden is the green amaranth, also known as pigweed. The dense green spike consists of many tiny inconspicuous flowers. The leaves are eaten in some parts of the world and the seeds, treated as grain and prized by the Aztecs, are high in protein. The plant comes from tropical America and is related to the popular flower, love-lies bleeding, with its long spectacular tassels of tiny red blooms.

Each of these three alien plant species are said to thrive in waste places which says nothing positive about my gardening abilities.

Eighteen Common Fungi

Fungi do not fit into either the animal or plant kingdoms so form a group of their own. There are many diverse kinds of these fascinating and mysterious organisms. Those I have illustrated were found in local woods and fields and are the fruiting bodies which produce spores by which they propagate. They do not have the green pigment chlorophyll, so are unable to make their own food as plants do. They derive nutrition from dead or decaying organic materials and are vital in the decomposition of organic material and nutrient recycling, thus making basic compounds available to plants. This is accomplished by a mass of thread-like processes (mycelium) that permeate the substrate on which the fruiting body grows.

Apart from the familiar mushroom type, fungi also includes yeasts, moulds and rusts. Yeast is necessary in bread making and in the fermentation of beers and wines. Some species glow in the dark, a phenomenon known as bioluminescence. Some fungi are parasitic on animals and plants, causing fruit to spoil for instance. Others cause illness in humans, ranging from mild upsets to fatalities, while some are used for treating illness. Most plant species depend upon a close (mycorrhizal) relationship with specific fungi for nutrition.

Mushrooms are grown commercially in the dark, but it has been found that exposing them to a little sunlight increases their vitamin D content significantly.

Beatrix Potter, the famous illustrator and children's writer, produced many accurate paintings of fungi. She became interested in how fungi reproduced, As a gifted amateur scientist, she worked on fungal spore germination and held theories about symbiotic relationships of some fungal species and algae to form lichens. Sadly, her work was not taken seriously by the exclusively male members of the Linnaean Society.

Birch polypore

Field mushroom

Shaggy ink cap

Stags horn

Calocera viscosa

King Alfred's cakes

Russula species

Parasol mushroom

Puffball species

Many-zoned polypore

Stinkhorn

Mycena species

Fly agaric

Jew's ear

Scarlet elf cup

Sulphur tuft

Orange peel fungus

Boletus species

Snipe

When holidaying in Northumberland we stopped near a large reservoir to look out for a great crested grebe we had seen earlier. Peeping over a wall at the side of the reservoir we noticed a small band of snipe, known as a 'wisp', not fifteen yards away. They were busily probing the soft mud.

The bill of the snipe is very long and the tip is both flexible and sensitive allowing the bird to locate hidden food items.

The birds were obviously unaware of our presence which gave me the opportunity to make several sketches from which this picture is composed.

Meadow saffron

I found these delicate flowers in damp woodland. They bloom in the autumn; the fruit and large leaves appear in the spring.

Like the crocus, the meadow saffron shows an extreme example of flower structure. The blooms are borne on weak tubular 'stalks' about 20 cms long which, in fact, are extensions of the conjoined petals. Unusually the ovary, which nurtures the seeds, is underground, therefore the style emerging from it, must be very long in order to hold the stigma at the same level as the petals.

These rare flowers are also known as naked ladies.

Red hedgerow fruit

The joy of a country walk in autumn is made more pleasurable by the brightly coloured fruit in the hedgerows.

Woody nightshade, or bittersweet, belongs to the same family as the potato and tomato. Its attractive purple and yellow flowers are followed by glossy poisonous red berries. The plant has been mistaken for the deadly nightshade whose berries are larger, borne singly and black.

Many wild fruits are poisonous or unpalatable. The berries of honeysuckle, black bryony, holly and the oddly-shaped fruit of spindle are all poisonous to humans but holly berries, which may remain on the tree until February, are eaten by birds. Hawthorn berries, also known as haws, are an important source of food for blackbirds, thrushes and overwintering fieldfares and redwings. Clusters of rowan berries are relished by flocks of visiting waxwings. The fleshy outer parts of yew berries are not poisonous but the seed within is.

There was a shortage of citrus fruit during World War 2. When it was realised that rose hips contained weight for weight, more vitamin C than oranges, families gathered them and a generation of children were given rose hip syrup.

As children we referred to the 'seeds' (achenes) within rose hips as itchy pills. When dropped down the back of the neck they cause the most irritating itching sensation.

Woody nightshade

Black bryony

Hawthorn

Spindle

Holly

Guelder
rose

Yew

Honeysuckle

Rowan

Field rose

185

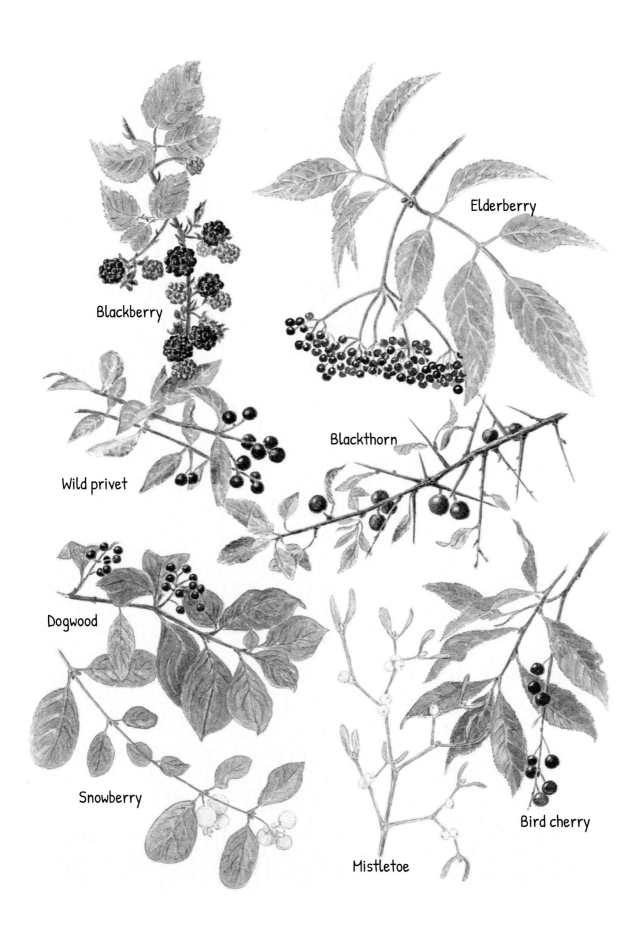

Blackberry

Elderberry

Wild privet

Blackthorn

Dogwood

Snowberry

Mistletoe

Bird cherry

186

Black fruit and white fruit

The fruit produced by these hedgerow plants is eaten by various animals, particularly birds. The fruit was also exploited historically by country people for food, home remedies and other utilitarian purposes.

Snowberry was planted as cover for game birds and the spongy white berries may last throughout the winter but are eaten by pheasants in the most severe weather. Mistletoe is taken by thrushes. The seeds are coated with a sticky substance which ensures they adhere to the tree bark when the bird wipes its beak. Privet, though poisonous to humans, is eaten by birds. The berries were once used to make dyes and dogwood berries were a source of lamp oil.

The plum-like fruit of bird cherry and blackthorn (sloes) have a single very hard stone and may sometimes be taken by birds. They have been used to flavour wines and sloe gin is well known. Blackberries make the most wonderful jellies and blackberry and apple jam has long been my favourite. A lovely light wine is easily made using elderflowers; it is only bettered by the superb elderberry wines.

More fruit

The functions of fruit is to protect the seeds and facilitate their dispersal.

A big seed, containing a relatively large store of nutrients, is better equipped than a small one to establish viable progeny. However, its greater bulk makes it more difficult to transport. Though smaller seeds contain less nutritious material to sustain the early growth of young plants, they are easier to disperse and are generally produced in greater numbers. During the course of evolution plants have evolved ways of striking a balance between these opposing factors.

When seed is shed, the ideal is to achieve a widespread scattering of individual seeds. Fruits of herb bennet, burdock and goosegrass have many hair-like processes ending in tiny hooks forming burrs which catch in animal fur. Squirrels and mice hide nuts on the forest floor and jays hide acorns. Inevitably, many are never relocated. Birds feeding on fleshy fruit may ingest hard seeds which pass through their digestive systems to be deposited some distance away.

As the pods of legumes like peas and birdsfoot trefoil dry, tensions are set up in their structures which, when suddenly released, result in the seeds being thrown out. Similarly when the mature fruits of Himalayan balsam are disturbed it bursts open explosively propelling its seeds several yards in a most dramatic way earning it the alternative name of touch-me-not.

Some seeds, for example wild clematis, groundsel, dandelion and willows, have hairy attachments and are dispersed by the wind while sycamore, lime and elm have winged seeds. Poppy seeds are scattered as the long stems sway in the breeze and the slightest breath of air disperses the dust-like seeds of orchids.

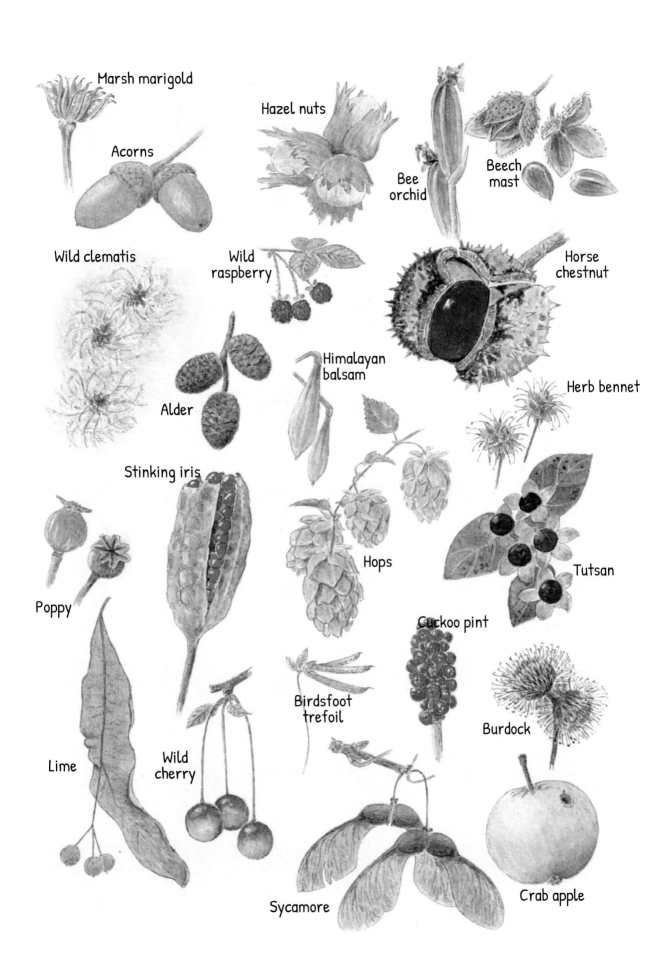

Marsh marigold

Acorns

Hazel nuts

Bee orchid

Beech mast

Wild clematis

Wild raspberry

Horse chestnut

Alder

Himalayan balsam

Herb bennet

Stinking iris

Hops

Tutsan

Poppy

Cuckoo pint

Birdsfoot trefoil

Burdock

Lime

Wild cherry

Sycamore

Crab apple

189

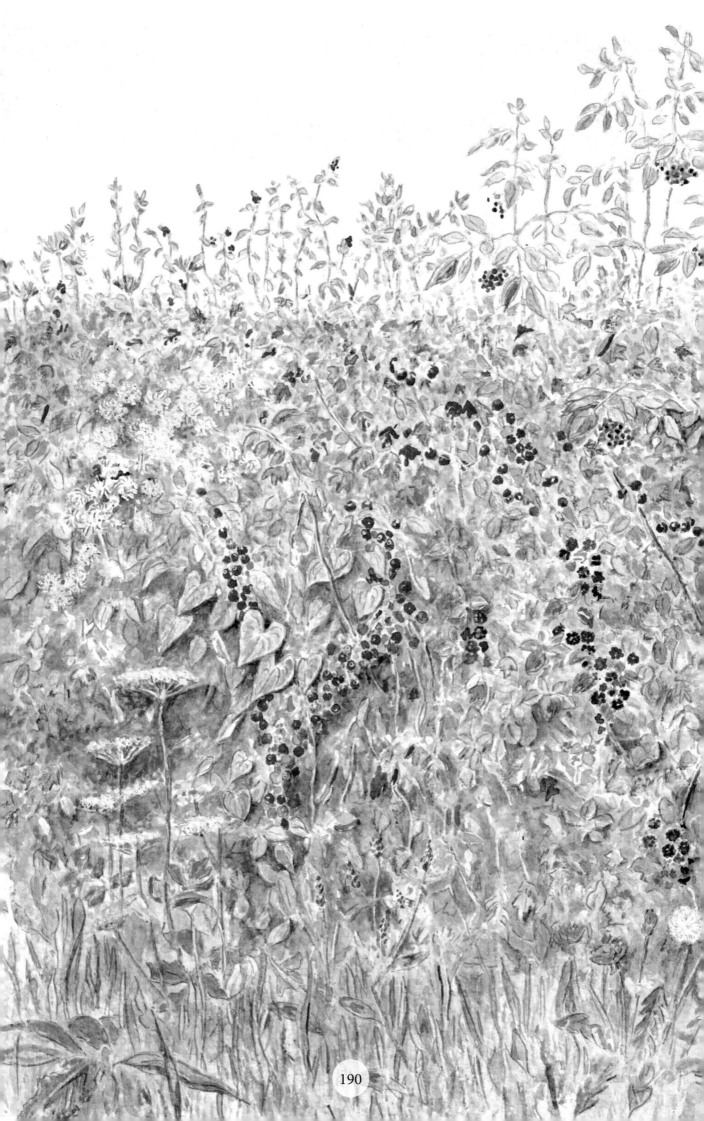

Hedges

This was painted during the season of 'fruitfulness' in late September. Small clusters of honeysuckle berries, with a few late flowers, can be seen at the tops of hedges. Fluffy grey fruit of old man's beard (wild clematis) contrast with crimson haws and green leaves. Strings of black bryony berries hang like necklaces; a few blackberries remain with remnants of elderberries, that lately hung in luscious bunches, spared by birds and wine makers. Further along the hedge one may see blackthorn with its plum-like sloes, bright red rose hips and the large white, almost luminous, hedge bindweed still in flower.

Some hedges are ancient, often marking parish boundaries; most are the result of 19th century enclosure acts. Hawthorn, also known as quickthorn, was planted with blackthorn to form stock proof boundaries. Elm and other large species were added to supply timber. Over time smaller trees and shrubs like hazel, elder, holly, dogwood, maple, spindle, and wayfaring trees, etc. found space to flourish within the hedge. Climbers such as ivy, woody nightshade, honeysuckle and bramble found a ready-made scaffold up which to scramble.

Wide dense hedges form wildlife corridors linking areas of fragmented woodland and constitute a rich habitat for a huge number and variety of creatures, supplying food, shelter and nesting sites. Litter accumulating at the base provides for vast numbers of invertebrates. Many wild flower species too, find conditions favourable on hedge banks and field margins.

In a drive to improve the efficiency of crop production about 75,000 miles of hedges were grubbed up from about 1945 to 1990 with the inevitable huge loss to nature. However, the vital importance of hedges for much of our wildlife has been recognised, and hedge planting is now encouraged.

The common shrew

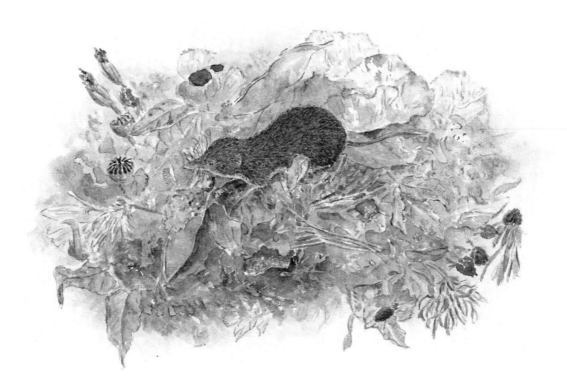

Lifting the cover off my garden compost bin I noticed a shrew which quickly ran away. Just beneath the surface litter of waste, the shrew would find food in abundance, worms, woodlice, insect larvae and other small invertebrates.

Due to the relatively large surface area to the volume of its body, the shrew, like all small animals, loses heat rapidly. It is essential therefore that it eats regularly. This need can only be satisfied by hunting, necessitating yet more food to fuel this activity. It uses its long pointed flexible snout to detect food. Some authorities state that the common shrew needs to consume 80% to 90% of its own body weight each day. The result is that this tiny animal hunts both day and night with only brief regular rests.

The presence of a shrew may be betrayed by its high-pitched squeaking, but it is rare to glimpse one alive, much more often it is seen dead, often on a footpath. Owls can cope with the distasteful flesh of shrews; cats kill them but will not eat them.

Hedge bindweed

This is a common hedgerow plant which, in contrast to the honeysuckle, climbs in an anticlockwise direction. Its flowers are among the largest found in Britain. They are pure white and spectacularly beautiful.

Two of its alternative names reflect different aspects of the plant. It is known as wild morning glory in some areas. Some gardeners know it as devil's guts, as its extensive root system makes it a persistent and vigorous weed and difficult to eradicate.

It would be better loved if it were less common.

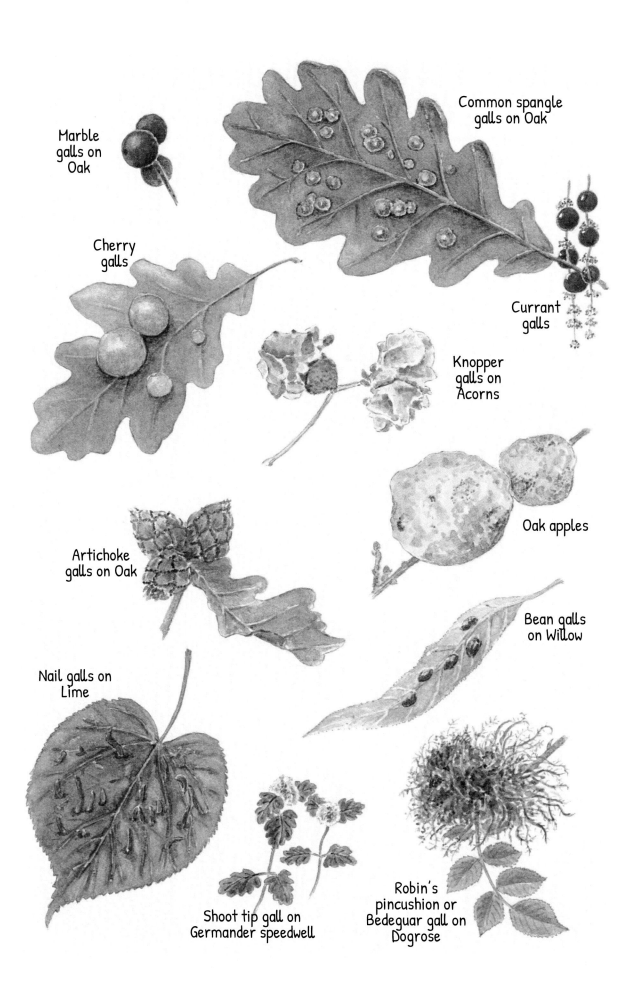

Marble galls on Oak

Common spangle galls on Oak

Cherry galls

Currant galls

Knopper galls on Acorns

Oak apples

Artichoke galls on Oak

Bean galls on Willow

Nail galls on Lime

Shoot tip gall on Germander speedwell

Robin's pincushion or Bedeguar gall on Dogrose

Mysterious galls

Galls occur in many forms and on many plant species. In Britain they are well known on roses, thistles and trees. It is thought that our native oaks are host to about 30 species. Galls are caused by gall wasps, gall gnats, various fungi and viruses and may appear on leaves, twigs and flower buds. Gall wasps have complex life cycles. The wasp responsible for the common spangle gall is an example.

In summer this tiny gall wasp lays fertilised eggs on the leaves of sessile and pedunculate oaks. Each larva secretes a chemical which induces an abnormal growth on the leaf resulting in the formation of a disc-like gall. The larvae develop within the galls which detach from the leaves and fall to the ground in September and October. They overwinter in the leaf litter where they develop further. A totally female generation of gall wasps emerge in the following spring. This generation of females lay unfertilised eggs on male oak catkins or sometimes on developing leaves. Galls, which look like currants, grow on the oak catkins, as illustrated, and a generation of male and female gall wasps emerge in June. They mate, and fertilised eggs are laid on oak leaves and the cycle begins again. There are actually several kinds of spangle galls found on oak leaves each caused by a different gall wasp species.

Knopper galls are sticky and first become noticeable in Britain in the 1960's. They are found on pedunculate oaks with a second generation developing on the catkins of Turkey oak. They spread rapidly causing serious concern that they would affect acorn fertility and thus our iconic oaks. However, no appreciable damage to plants appears to have been caused by the activities of gall wasps.

Oak galls contain tannin and marble galls were used for many centuries to make a reliable waterproof ink.

Ivy in October

Ivy is a very common woody evergreen climber. Short aerial roots, which do not take sustenance from the tree, rocks or walls up which its climbs, cling tenaciously enabling the plant to reach heights of 20 metres or more. It is often a dominant species in hedges also.

Ivy produces flowers and fruit when little else is available for insects and birds. It flowers from about October to November delivering copious quantities of nectar which attracts numerous insect species including bees, wasps, late butterflies and especially hover flies. As the insects move over the flowers they effect pollination.

The dark, almost black, fruits that develop are ripe by midwinter and may be available until March or April. They are poisonous to humans but are a very valuable food source for blackbirds, thrushes and wood pigeons.

Ivy forms a dense tangle of glossy leaves throughout the winter in which many insects, also small birds, shelter. Brimstone butterflies tend to hide among the leaves of ivy to hibernate and the larvae of some moth species eat the leaves. When spring arrives birds find the cover provided by ivy a convenient and relatively safe place to nest.

Altogether ivy is indeed a very important plant for wildlife.

The fox

Foxes are largely nocturnal. They are resourceful and readily adapt to almost any environment. A Ministry of Agriculture investigation into the stomach contents of dead foxes showed that their main food items were rats, mice and voles. They also prey on hedgehogs, squirrels, frogs, rabbits and birds and will eat snails, beetles and berries. They will raid the unprotected chicken run too!

I saw this fox very early one morning. I was a short distance behind it and it seemed unaware of me. It crept slowly towards an old wall when a handsome cock pheasant fluttered up to the top of the wall clearly aware of the fox and its intentions. The fox no doubt was salivating, while the pheasant seemed confident of its security atop the wall. After a period of stealthy manoeuvring the fox, realising it was unable to exercise sufficient craft, for which its tribe is notorious, in order to ensure a luxurious feast, quietly trotted away to seek a bite elsewhere- or go hungry.

Autumn leaves

The green colour of leaves is due to chlorophyll. Chlorophyll traps the energy of sunlight to synthesise carbohydrates from carbon dioxide and water, releasing oxygen. The process is known as photosynthesis. Green leaves are therefore nature's food factories and, as such, are at the base of food chains.

With cooler weather of autumn profound changes occur in the natural world throughout temperate regions. Bird migration is underway, mammals and insects prepare for winter and many plants shut down too.

The leaves of evergreens are well equipped to survive, being tough, thick and waxy. They may remain on the trees for several years before they eventually fall and decompose.

As winter approaches food substances in the leaves of deciduous trees are transported into the main body of the plant and the green pigment chlorophyll, which played such a vital role in the manufacture of food materials, breaks down. It is then that other pigments show prominently, yellows, oranges, browns, reds and purple. A corky layer forms where each leaf breaks away sealing plants against attack by fungi. The leaves eventually fall to the ground. Here a host of leaf litter animals, the vital heroes of recycling, get to work in silence and unsung, slugs and snails, beetles and flies and their larvae, earthworms, woodlice, millipedes, springtails, also bacteria and fungi, decomposing the spent leaves into basic materials that plants can use again.

Amazing though the science is, what childish pleasure can be gained on a sunny autumn morning kicking one's way through carpets of beautiful fallen leaves. Often a lone robin will be following behind picking up invertebrates disturbed in the leaf litter.

Hazel

Wild service

Birch

Lime

Sweet
chestnut

Pedunculate or
English oak

Hawthorn

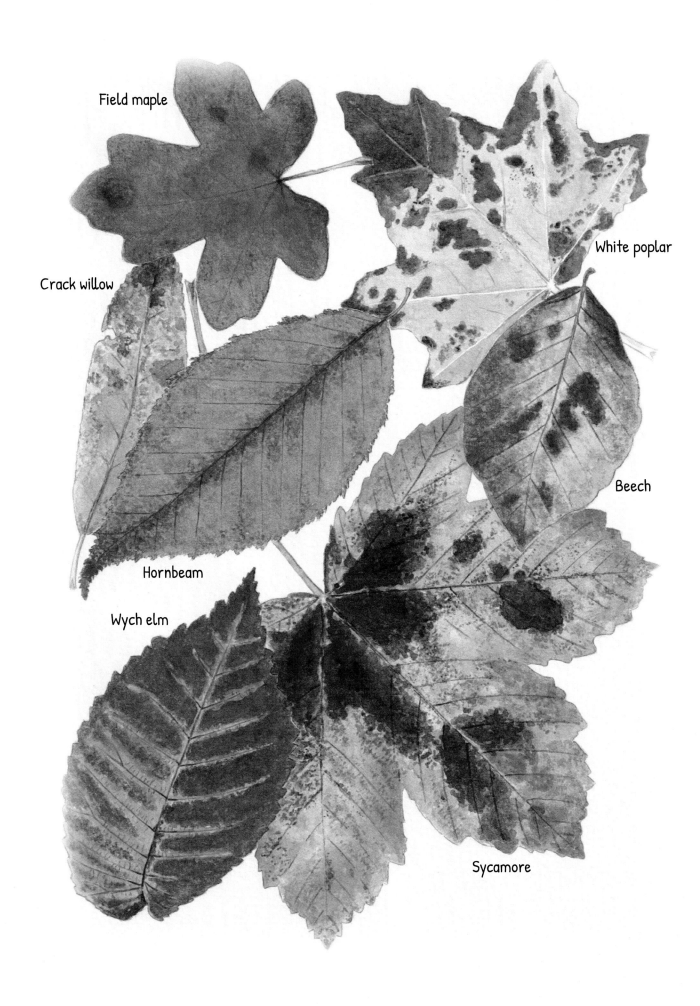

Field maple

White poplar

Crack willow

Beech

Hornbeam

Wych elm

Sycamore

Fieldfares and Redwings

Arriving in October and November these members of the thrush family migrate from the colder climates of Scandinavia and Northern Europe. Both birds take worms, insects, insect larvae and wild fruit. Sadly the flailing of hedgerows has resulted in far fewer berries available for birds. Flocks of these two birds may be seen in winter feeding together in fields and orchards where they relish windfall apples, fieldfares outnumbering redwings by about three to one. They are gregarious birds chattering constantly.

The head and rump of the fieldfare is usually described as grey in colour. But when seen with winter sunshine on its back, the colour appears as a beautiful mauve.

Waxwings on rowan

Waxwings are not native to Britain but nest in Scandinavian and Russian forests. From time to time flocks visit Britain in winter when, perhaps, there is a shortage of berries in their northern breeding grounds. The winter of 2011-12 was a 'waxwing winter' when very many birds arrived and were seen as far inland as the West Midlands.

They are gregarious birds flocking together to feed on berries of holly, guelder rose and hawthorn. Perhaps their favourite food is rowan berries.

Waxwings are reported as flying into windows more than most other birds. This may have fatal consequences and indeed my young granddaughter found a dead bird. We had mixed feelings for, while we regretted the death of such a beautiful bird, we were able to examine it closely and see the 'sealing wax' blobs at the ends of its secondary flight feathers which gives this attractive bird its name.

Cones

In general, male and female flowers of conifers are borne on the same trees. Pollen produced by male flowers is carried by the wind to fertilise the ovules of the female flowers. As the seeds grow, the female flower develops into the familiar woody cone that we all recognise.

The scales of cones are arranged in spirals. On spruce and pine cones one can count thirteen spirals going one way and eight in the opposite direction. These are consecutive numbers of the Fibonacci series, a sequence of numbers relating to many examples found in the natural world, such as the closely packed florets in the centre of daisies.

The scales of mature cones remain closed in cold damp weather, opening when it is warm and dry. It is then that the seeds are released to be carried off on the breeze.

Illustrated with the cone of the Norway spruce are two winged seeds, shown enlarged, two being the number found beneath each scale of the cone.

Squirrels may strip cones off trees to take the nutritious seeds and crossbills, as their names suggest, have specially adapted bills enabling them to extract seeds from beneath the scales.

Most of our conifers are introductions, only juniper, yew and Scot's pine are native species. Larch is deciduous, shedding its needles in autumn and remaining leafless until spring. Yew is a conifer, though it doesn't have conventional cones; its seeds are enclosed in fleshy, red berry-like structures known as arils. The Norway spruce is perhaps, our best known conifer as it is our traditional Christmas tree.

The crushed needles of most conifers have distinctive smells. The Norway spruce has a scent I find hard to describe, my favourite though, is the strong citrus aroma of the Douglas fir.

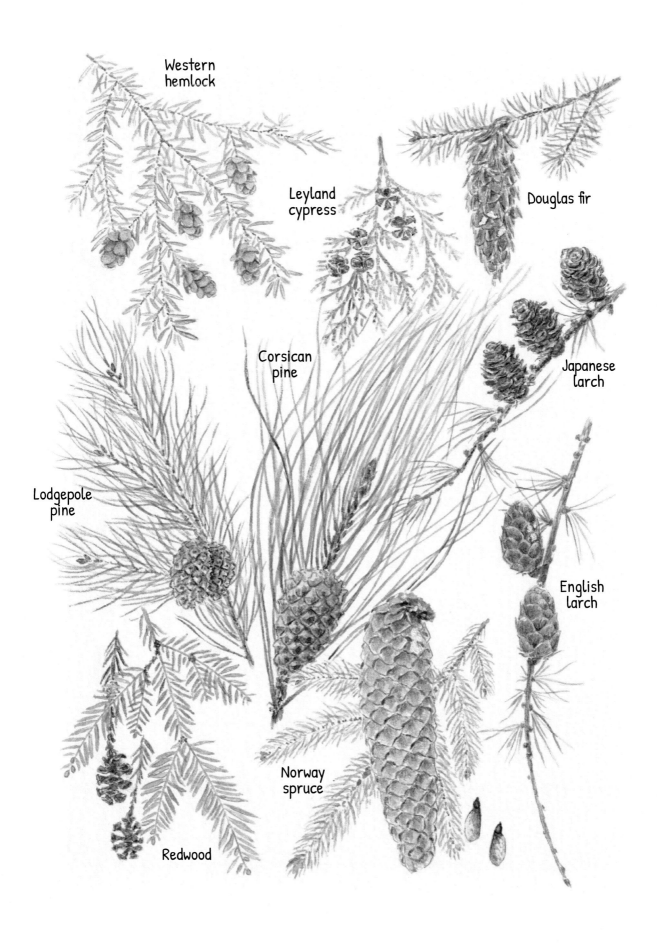

Western
hemlock

Leyland
cypress

Douglas fir

Corsican
pine

Japanese
larch

Lodgepole
pine

English
larch

Redwood

Norway
spruce

Goldcrest

Barely 8 cms long, the goldcrest is our smallest bird. It is very active and one or two can often be seen foraging with a band of tits in deciduous woodland for tiny insects and spiders. Its real niche though, is among conifers. I saw this tiny bird in a plantation of mature Douglas firs in December and thought about its chances of surviving the winter. Birds need to maintain a core temperature a few degrees warmer than us, but due to its high surface area to volume ratio, the goldcrest is vulnerable to the cold. Birds tend to gorge in autumn, creating insulating fat reserves. Some species roost alone, others communally. They seek a sheltered spot, fluff up their feathers, creating insulating air pockets, and tend to sit on their feet. Birds can reduce the blood flow to their feet and a heat exchange system minimises heat loss from them. Nevertheless, many goldcrests die in severe winters, though numbers soon recover for they may lay up to 10 eggs.

Hibernating dormouse

In the days when farm workers maintained hedges and ditches by hand, they used to find these delightful little animals and children kept them as pets. Management of hedges is now mechanised, more importantly, many hedges have been removed. These two factors contribute to the present rarity of dormice.

A friend who was licensed to handle dormice, once found a hibernating dormouse in his garden. The nest was not perfectly dry, as we had expected, but fairly damp. Dormice usually hibernate in the leaf litter at the bottom of a hedge or other dense vegetation which, of course, is invariably moist. When hibernating, the heart rate, temperature and respiration rates fall. Nevertheless, the little animal must breathe and in doing so loses moisture which, over a period of 5 or 6 months hibernation, could leave the dormouse fatally dehydrated. Covering its nose with its tail during hibernation would appear to help in retaining moisture.

After thoughts

I was lucky to have had an early introduction to the delights of our wonderful natural world. Sadly however, there now appears to be a diminishing recognition of the values of nature in promoting good health, for its huge economic benefits and indeed, for its own sake. There are many distractions of course. We can enjoy a version of nature on our television screens and be captivated by incredible films from wildlife hot spots and managed reserves brought to us by huge production teams using state of the art technology and presented by acknowledged experts with privileged access.

Essentially it is poor substitute for the real experience and does little to address the problems.

The subliminal message is, 'get out there for there are plenty of these marvels for you to see for yourself'. But 'plenty' is a comparative term. Sadly, the most relevant word is 'decline'; a serious decline in both numbers and species of animals and plants.

A report, The State of Nature 2016, compiled by an august group of organisations including the RSPB, the National Trust and Natural History Museum, stated that the U.K. is one of the 'most nature-depleted countries in the world' with more than half of our species in decline and one in seven facing extinction. The issue is complex. The principal causes are considered to be habitat loss, urbanisation, climate change and farming intensification, to which I would add public apathy and councils' drive for sterile tidiness and inability to recognise the importance of nature in our lives. Of course conservation bodies, recognising the problems, are working to reverse the trends and have achieved some notable successes.

Certainly, from the time I was a boy, I have witnessed a distressing reduction in the number and variety of animals and plants in the area I have been familiar with for many decades. Hares, water voles, bats, even hedgehogs, frogs and toads are now scarce. I miss the ponds, the banks smothered with primroses, the field corners where cowslips and a few orchids grew. I miss the species-rich wild flower meadows with their hundreds of colourful butterflies and buzzing insects. I miss the bird song.

The glorious, enchanting outpouring of the skylark's song was once an evocation that all was well with the natural world, its demise tells a different story.

I fear that today many people, particularly the young, have no engagement with our health-promoting natural world. Children are being denied because governments do not appear to ascribe any value to practical outdoor environmental education. With very little knowledge of nature, children, unable to evaluate the vital importance of natural systems and with only a limited appreciation of the vast benefits nature bestows on us, may consider it to be of little value and not worth protecting.

Outdoor environmental education is vital. We simply cannot be so irresponsible as to put the stewardship of our unique planet, on which we all ultimately depend, into the hands of a generation with no real experience of the countryside.

Bernard Kear

April 2021

Acknowledgements

First of all I am grateful to my father for opening my eyes to the wonders of the natural world. I am grateful also to friends who helped with useful information and encouragement, notably, Trevor Roach, Steve Kirk, Pat and John Fletcher, Cheryl Mayo and also David Harris for dealing with the mysteries of electronic technology. Special thanks to Averil Kear for typing my notes and pushing the project along. I thank my wife Pauline for her enthusiasm and patience and my family for their encouragement. Perhaps the greatest inspiration comes from the children I have met who, given the opportunity, delight in the scientific and aesthetic aspects of nature.

Bibliography

Work I have found useful for information and inspiration include:-

British Trees in Colour. By Cyril Hart and Charles Raymond. (Book Club Associates)

Clare, Selected Poems and Prose. Eric Robinson and Geoffrey Summerfield. (Oxford University Press)

Collins Guide to British Insects. By Michael Chinery. (Collins)

Flowers and Their Visitors. By Janet Davidson. (Adam and Charles Black)

Saving Planet Earth. By Tony Juniper (Harper Collins)

Sketches of Dean's Birds. By John Christian (Magpie Publishing)

The Country Diary of an Edwardian Lady. By Edith Holden (Michael Joseph)

The Secret Life of Flowers. By Anne Ophelia Dowden (Paul Hamlyn)

The Wild Garden. By Lys de Bray (Weidenfeld and Nicolson)

Weeds. By Richard Mabey (Profile Books)

Wild Animals of the British Isles. By Maurice Burton (Frederick Warne)

INDEX

INDEX

INDEX